Portraits

*Testimonies from graduates of the
Latin American Biblical University*

Portraits

Testimonies from graduates of the Latin American Biblical University

Janet W. May
Editor

UNIVERSIDAD BÍBLICA LATINOAMERICANA
SAN JOSÉ, COSTA RICA

www.ubila.net

Portraits

Testimonies from graduates of the Latin American Biblical University

Janet W. May, Editor

Publisher: Avecilla

Editor: May Janet W.

Cover design: May Janet W.

Translator: May Robert A.

As told by: Ramírez Arístides, Adames Digna, Blanco Coralia, Roman Ángel, Madrigal Larry, López Azucena, Tamez Elsa, Chinchilla Eduardo, Dell Marlen, Fonseca Nidia, Yucra Dorotea, Murray Julio, Quevedo Élida, Viracocha Blanca, Llanco César, Quezada Luzmila, Alanoca German, Rosas Yolanda, Moreira Silva Maria do Carmo, Lais Tourn Margarita

ISBN-10: 0981943306

ISBN-13: 9780981943305

Subject: Religion

Website URL: www.ubila.net

DOI: http://www.usdoi.org/index.php?page=DetailsXML&doi=http://www.usdoi.org/index.php?page=DetailsXML&doi=10.1604/9780981943305

Description: How do people experience a call to ministry? Why do they go to seminary? These interviews with graduates of the Latin American Biblical University answer these questions and more. They may even inspire you to study your own religious tradition.

This published work and its content is copyright of Janet May - © www.ubila.net, 2008. All rights reserved world wide.

All trademarks and servicemarks are property of their respective owners. Any redistribution or reproduction of part or all of the contents in any form is prohibited other than the following: You may copy extracts for your personal and non-commercial use only.

You may not, except with our express written permission, distribute or commercially exploit the content. Nor may you transmit it or store it in any other website or other form of electronic retrieval system.

The information contained in this book is the opinion of the editor and the contributors. Neither Janet May, the contributors or the Latin American Biblical University assume any liability whatsoever for the use of or inability to use any or all of the information contained in this publication.

Use this information at your own risk.

Proceeds from this book are designated to the Universidad Bíblica Latinoamericana.

*To my students and friends at the
Universidad Bíblica Latinoamericana*

Contents

Introduction 5

Aristides Ramírez
Dominican Republic, Pentecostal 9

Digna Adames
Dominican Republic, Roman Catholic 13

Coralia Blanco
Cuba, Baptist 17

Ángel Román
Guatemala, Episcopal 21

Larry Madrigal
El Salvador, Independent 25

Azucena López
Nicaragua, Church of God 29

Elsa Tamez
Mexico and Costa Rica, Presbyterian and Methodist 33

Eduardo Chinchilla
Costa Rica, Methodist 37

Marlen Dell
Costa Rica, Baptist … 45

Nidia Fonseca
Costa Rica, Methodist … 49

Dorotea Yucra
Peru and Costa Rica, Independent … 59

Julio Murray
Panama, Episcopal … 63

Élida Quevedo
Venezuela, Pentecostal … 69

Blanca Viracocha
Ecuador, Methodist … 73

César Llanco
Peru, Methodist … 75

Luzmila Quezada
Peru, Wesleyan … 79

Germán Alanoca
Bolivia, Methodist … 83

Yolanda Rosas
El Salvador, Guatemala and Bolivia, Mennonite and Pentecostal … 87

María do Carmo Moreira Silva
Brazil, Methodist … 91

Margarita Lais Tourn
Argentina, Waldensian … 95

Portraits! | Janet W. May, Editor

The UBL and sister institutions

Map Copyright © 2008 Digital Vector Maps

UBL = university-level program   IBP = Biblical Pastoral Institute (non-university program)

1 USA: Nashville, TN, General Board of Higher Education and Ordained Ministry of the United Methodist Church, UBL
2 Cuba: Havana, Dr. Martin Luther King, Jr. Memorial Center, UBL
3 Dominican Republic: Santo Domingo, ISEBID, a study program organized by four institutions: the Baptist Seminary, the Theological Study Center of

the Episcopal Church, The Ecumenical School of Biblical Sciences (Roman Catholic) and the Biblical Seminary of the Church of God. All are university level.

4 Mexico: Chiapas, Mayan Cultural Center, IBP and the Indígenous Program. They are revising our university level curriculum in view of participation.

5 Guatemala: Quetzaltenango, IBP, Fraternity of Mayan Presbyteries. Guatemala City: CEDEPCA. IBP and UBL.

6 Honduras: Tegucigalpa, Honduran Theological Community: IBP, UBL

7 Nicaragua: Bluefields, Moravian Theological Seminary, IBP, and with future plans to cooperate at the UBL level

8 Costa Rica: IBP: the Episcopal Church Center at La Guácima, the Baptist Seminary, the National Pain and Paliative Care Clinic. The Baptist Seminary is also holding dialogue on cooperation at the UBL level.

9 Venezuela: UEPV at the IBP level. Conversations are being held with SOBICAIN (Catholic) and with the Lutheran Church, at the UBL level

10 Colombia: Bogotá, PROMESA, American School and the Mennonite Seminary, all at the UBL level

11 Ecuador: Quito, conversations with the Episcopal Church, the Methodist Church and the Mennonite Church at the UBL level and in Riobamba, the Evangelical Indigenous Federation works with the IBP level and the Indigenous Program as well as exploring possible UBL-level programs

12 Peru: Huancayo, San Pablo Seminary with the UBL, IBP y Indigenous Program; Cusco, SEBITEM with IBP and the Indigenous Program; Chiclayo, Pilgrim Seminary at the UBL level y Lima with IBP and UBL levels

13 Bolivia: La Paz, ISEAT, the Andean Ecumenical Theological Institute of Higher Education, UBL

14 Chile: Concepción, Evangelical Center of Pentecostal Studies, IBP and UBL.

Portraits! | Janet W. May, Editor

Introduction

The Latin American Biblical University (UBL) has one of the largest campuses in the world, spanning two continents. From its center in San José, Costa Rica, the theological education program of the UBL is carried out in 19 study centers in 14 countries, at both university and non-degree levels. It is widely recognized as one of the principal theological study programs in Latin America and the Caribbean, training pastors and laity for the growing Christian communities that give testimony and service throughout the region.

The university was founded as a women's Bible Institute in 1923 and has stood out for its creativity in the development of educational models for theological education. By 1930 there was a group of 40 men and women students from eleven countries: Colombia, Puerto Rico, Cuba, Bolivia, Peru, Guatemala, El Salvador, Honduras, Nicaragua, Panama and Costa Rica. In 1934, the Biblical Institute launched an extension education program, through correspondence courses. In 1954, The Institute became the Latin American Biblical Seminary (SBL) In 1971, the SBL became an independent institution, no longer governed by a mission agency. Agreements with the University of Costa Rica in 1972 and with the National University in 1976 reflect the high level of academic quality maintained by the seminary.

Another important step was the birth of study centers affiliated with the seminary. The first center was formed in Bolivia in 1983, where students who had previous studied independently gathered and took courses with materials developed by the seminary. This center still exists. Although it has passed through several transformations since it named itself the Theological Study Center, it continues as a part of the network and is now known as ISEAT. This impulse to form groups grew and in 1990 the SBL launched a diversified, decentralized, integrated and contextual theological program. In 1997, the SBL once again underwent a transformation, becoming the Latin American Biblical University, or UBL, according to its initials in Spanish.

In the mid-1980s, the SBL launched a non-degree study program to serve the needs of many pastors and leaders who were unable to enter university-level programs. This led to the consolidation of the Biblical Pastoral Institute, or IBP, in 1997. This program offers study materials, training and the accompaniment of church leaders throughout Latin America and the Caribbean.

The UBL has students and professors from the mainstream historical Protestant denominations, the Roman Catholic Church, pentecostal churches and independent evangelical church organizations. The institution finds itself becoming more and more ecumenical as it seeks to respond to the concrete needs of the growing number of churches in the region. The center of its life and growth is a diversified teaching model that is highly regarded around the world and is being adopted by a growing number of seminaries.

Having accomplished ten years of work as a government-accredited university, the UBL has entered a polyfacetic evaluation program. In 2006, the UBL initiated a strategic planning process, guided by CREAS, a South American ecumenical organization. Since the beginning of this process, the UBL has developed a clear vision and mission statement. The vision: the UBL as a consolidated theological program that offers educational programs that are pertinent to the churches and social movements in Latin America and the Caribbean, contributing to the construction of societies where there is social equality, enjoyment and the practice of peace with justice, founded on faith as a living guidepost for practice. The Mission: the UBL is an ecumenical Latin American and Caribbean theological education institution that, beginning with theological reflection and research, contributes to the strenthening of transformative processes in the churches and in society. With the commitment to promote equality and the full participation of all men and women in all of their diversity, according to the vision we have experienced of the presence in society of the Reign of God, the UBL works out its mission through connections with a network of educational institutions.

Among many elements of the UBL's evaluative process, we decided to talk to graduates and former students who had chosen the UBL as their place to study theology. For these interviews, the UBL sought to include a diversity of voices from different countries, denominations and cultural groups. We included people in different ministries, such as local pastorates, formal and nonformal theological education, collaborators with ecumenical groups and agencies. We included men and women, actual students and graduates, both from recent years and from the past. Taking into account the rich heritage of eight decades of labor, we have included people both from the Seminary period and from the University program.

The interviews were open-ended, taking into account six basic points: 1) name, place of work and something about the person's pastoral experience; 2) how did he or she decide to study theology?; 3) what importance or impact did theological study have on the way in which they carried out ministry?; 4) an example of a pastoral experience that they have had in which their training has been relevant; 5) pending dreams, personal and pastoral, and 6) what advice would they give to somebody who wanted to explore the possibility of studying theology. We have respected the individual style of each interviewee although we have deleted the questions and, in some cases, edited the lenth of the interviews. We then decided to organize the interviews from north to south, beginning with the Caribbean.

The interviews reveal common threads. The UBL is perceived as a place where there is intellectual freedom, where students are encouraged to question and to search for answers, without denomination doctrinal restrictions, while at the same time respecting historical wisdom. The students are men and women who seek to connect faith and daily living. They seek out opportunities to know people from other countries, cultures and faith traditions. They are socially committed, with a great desire to learn and to share what they have learned.

Let me add a personal note: I, too, am a graduate of the SBL. Indeed, I'm among the first twelve people to receive a Bachelor's degree through the SBL's distance learning program known as PRODIADIS. The UBL is "my" institution and I greatly value it. So the stories presented here are also "my" story.

I thank all who contributed to making this dream come true: Violeta Rocha, the Rector of the UBL, who assigned me the project; my husband, Roy, whose support and insistence were vital to finishing. I thank Sergio Talero and Patricia Zúñiga for their hours and hours of listening to tapes and typing each word. I also thank Sergio for interviewing Marlen Dell, with whom I was never able to connect. I owe a special thanks to my son Robert who translated everything from Spanish to English. I thank Dámaris Álvarez for her assistence with layout and for correcting my technical and linguistic errors in Spanish. And I thank each and every person that was interviewed. Without everybody's contribution, this project would never have happened.

Janet May

San José, Costa Rica
2008

Much of the historical information about the UBL is adapted from the website www.ubila.org.

Portraits! | Janet W. May, Editor

Janet W. May, Editor | Portraits

Arístides Ramírez
Dominican Republic, Pentecostal

My name is Arístides Ramírez. I work in the Church of God in the Dominican Republic. The pastoral ministry in which I work is in a community. We have a group of twelve children with youth activities. In addition, we plan to do some handicraft work. At the general level of the church, I am working in a department that serves as a liaison with church professionals to offer their talents in ministry. There, I plan activities, medical services, and other proposals on social conditions that professionals in the future may propose to the Bishop. We are working on a directory of all professionals in the church, to know what social resources we have to offer to communities.

I collaborate as a teacher at the local Bible Seminary, and I am working with the rector of the seminary to assist with the UBL's program. I help in the registrar's office and also work to bring together four groups in the Dominican Republic to cooperate in theological education. My big dream in theology is to work in the area of accompaniment of pastors and their families, because I feel that often there is little confidence in pastoral accompaniment that is liberating, and, in turn is attached to ethical elements. I think pastors resist because they do not have people who are reliable. This has challenged me to combine my training as a psychologist and as a pastor.

It is a challenge to be a psychologist and minister of the church. As a pastor I seek to reach the community where I am assigned. I believe, that of the great dreams that I have, God has given me great blessings in the ministry because I

Portraits! | Janet W. May, Editor

Aristedes Ramirez

have always wanted to participate in what is practical theology. No one wants to stay with just the theoretical concepts but to work with the community and this has challenged me. Before, I had a lot of knowledge but I wasn't applying it to community service. Now they call me from the Catholic Church in my community about social problems in homes. Last Sunday, the lay leader called me to participate in the birthday of his daughter and I gave a prayer. All this helps me see a different dimension of the ministry, something that I did not see before. Before, I simply went to a place, gave a lecture, read a Bible text, participated in a service, but I did not always have the experience that a person would approach me and ask me to assist them and pray for their family. That has been a distinct dimension to the ministry.

I decided to study theology because of the many noble and motivating people who saw potential in me. On one occasion I was working on a counseling program and met a person who motivated me to study theology at a university in my country. He said that I had the vocation for teaching. I worked in the corporate sector as an organizational psychologist in the area of human resources. After twelve years working in the corporate sector, I realized that I had to put my talent into the hands of God. I was more into the atmosphere of productivity, but I felt that it was God who started to bless me in the spiritual area. I began to participate in a church and gained the bishop's confidence. I went to seminary, teaching at the Evangelical University of the Dominican Republic. I took courses in theology and I taught courses in psychology, that is how I got started. When the bishop invited me to the seminary, it was because he had been in contact with the rector of the university who suggested that I could make a contribution. The bishop gave me the opportunity and when the UBL's program was started, he understood that the Dominican Republic needed to strengthen theological studies in a more ecumenical character with the participation of historical groups. He understood that it was not a systematic theoretical theology, but a new and distinct theological approach, preparing pastors to serve as resources to support the community. I'm taking advantage of that opportunity, not so that I can say that I am going to have a degree, but to prepare for service in local communities, to serve for any social need that the country may need. Despite many opportunities, I have remained in my country and from here I serve the ministry. God has led me to understand that when a heart is noble and holy and is ready to serve, he will be responsible for blessing one's life. I've simply seen God's gratitude and his love upon my life. I did not go into the ministry because I wanted to make a living, I entered the ministry because I understood that God's mercy was great on my family and since God has been so good to me, I felt that everything I do has to be based on an interest in the welfare of humanity. I understand that God chose me, he could have chosen Peter or perhaps a madman who walks the street with a confused mind. The difference between that madman, Peter and me is that the grace of God came to me and I have to finish this task that God has entrusted to me.

In theological studies, I have been impacted by many lovely lessons, but there was one moment that deeply impacted me. Jose Duque went to the Dominican Republic and spoke a lot about people who have given their lives in ministry. He said that the Reign of God needed people who had the gift of science and wisdom, so that they could interpret the signs of the times. That challenged me to make a passionate commitment to theological work. I think that today's church is going through a very strong experience of renovation; there are churches that are profoundly shifting their identity; their educational process is weakening, because they emphasize many things, but I believe that God needs men and women who have the wisdom and vision to be able to encourage and assist.

At another point, I told Guido Mahecha* that I worked hard on a paper that I wrote for him, and I thought it would be very good, but he told me that since I already had a bachelor's degree in theology, he expected more from me. At the time I felt small in my state of mind because I expected better results, but something motivated me. When Guido saw I was a bit agitated, he taught me. He took it in great humor and told me to calm down. When he told me that, I calmed down and left it at that, because I understood that it was a challenge. When you're better prepared, you are expected to do more and I understood that I had to try harder, in a plane of growth. Guido is a great man and he was very supportive of me as a human being and the Dominican group, and after that day I felt so bad because it was not the grade, but the quality of work that had to improve. This incident shocked me. It has helped me because I'm told that I'm very patient, but sometimes I don't feel that way. One of the things that I have worked on in my character is emotional self-control, so as not to hurt anyone. It has helped me a lot to understand that intellectual intelligence is not the happiness of mankind, but it is the combination of emotional and intellectual intelligence that is important, because many times you can be very intellectual and a disaster as a human being. You can be very intelligent but perhaps someone who has a lower profile can be better in ministry, in work and family. So I try to develop a balance.

My advice to people who are thinking of studying theology is that every person has to be spontaneous in what is their vocation. I can never tell a person to study theology because it is going to get them a job in their denomination or

Guido Mahecha is a graduate and professor at the UBL.

project them in a field. People study something because they want to grow, both personally and spiritually. I believe that studying theology must be authentic, something you like, because in my country people have the mentality that theologians do not get jobs. They see us as passionate people who write a lot, but aren't needed in any productive way. So, I tell the youth to do so if that is their calling. I warn not to do it for the wrong reasons, thinking that in the future it'll be a jumping point to better living conditions. I tell them that I believe that no matter what career one studies, that it is important to explore their passion. That's what Howard Gardner says about multiple intelligences, that every person has to feel satisfaction in what they do. If I see that a young person doesn't like theology, then they won't be good ministers. I think that everyone who studies theology at the UBL must have an understanding of people, because the practice of pastoral theology or a pastoral ministry is not the same as academic research. Learning opens doors to understanding things in new ways, ways that we are not taught in church. There are many people who are confronted and I have seen them react emotionally, blocking themselves, because they are not prepared. So if I know that there someone who is not prepared to go into this new theological level, I would suggest they look into the Pastoral Bible Institute, to study in a program to strengthen their theological foundations. I would not send them to the university level, because it could be a traumatic experience in their life. That is my personal opinion.

Janet W. May, Editor | Portraits

Digna Adames

Dominican Republic, Roman Catholic

My name is Digna María Adámes. I'm from the Dominican Republic. I come from a Catholic tradition with an ecumenical spirit and I've been a member of a religious order for eighteen years. I have had a ministry that has a lot of work in the neighborhoods of the city of Santo Domingo. I do pastoral work, primarily in parishes that are very committed to liberation theology and in neighborhoods with a harsh social reality and a theology that is committed to the participation and training of the laity. There I have been actively involved in various ministries in the parishes. Over the past few years I was working with the Haitian ministry in Santo Domingo and in the rural areas. It is mostly social work, but at other times I was very involved with congregations in the area of training of young girls. Mostly, however, my work is a combination of pastoral and social work, mainly with migrants.

A specific area of ministry has been the biblical formation within the parish and in the Dominican Ecumenical Bible Network. I also lead Bible studies in local groups. I feel like I was sent to study by the base ecclesial communities of Santo Domingo because we felt the need for someone in the group to be trained in order to further enrich our work. Sometimes it seems like the well runs dry at the source and that it is necessary to renew and deepen it some more. That's why I came here. My dream always was to immerse myself into theology, as a consecrated woman in the Catholic church, and feeling the need for training.

Portraits! | Janet W. May, Editor
Digna Adames

That's why I studied philosophy first, thinking it was pre-requisite to study theology, and finally I came to study theology.

I think that I have had several vital experiences. I came to the Universidad Bíblica, first of all, because of its Latin American character, it's ecumenical dimension and its theology comes from its Latin American roots. In that sense, for me, it has been a very grateful and very rewarding experience, with a view to the future. I think that my ecumenical horizon has been broadened. And above all, it is deepening.

During this time I have also gone through the process of leaving the religious order. I feel like that horizon has become ecumenical as well, as a vital experience. It has been nurturing to be in contact with Latin American theology, and also with people who have been very close and supportive in the process of working on a Licenciature and now a Master's thesis. It is a gratifying enrichment of my human and Christian process in this Latin American reality.

I have always wanted to combine my practice of ministry with academic studies. I am very much inclined towards the sociological study of biblical texts. I have wanted to make connections between what I discover in the Bible and the faces, the people, the concrete community where I come from. I feel that this is necessary in order to enrich the biblical work in those communities. I have wanted to do this in everything - the research papers for the final course projects, and the thesis and dissertation work. It has to do with the link between Bible study and sociological study. I feel it has deepened my practice and I have been nourished and enriched academically.

As for dreams for the future, this is a tricky question. I'm in a time of redefinition of many things in my life. The first dream is to return to the community and reorient myself to that reality with this new training, trying to make it a rewarding process for the community. Lately, I have been greatly fueled by the dream of continuing academic studies and perhaps pursue a doctorate. It is still not very clear, but it is like a dream to continue learning in order to strengthen my practice.

One thing that I have always given as advice for those who want to study theology is that academic knowledge is always important for effective ministry. I think that going to seminary or university makes sense in so far as feeding practice, and not to nurture dreams of grandeur, or scaling the social and theological ladder, but for strengthening one's concrete commitment to the community. One should want to encourage people to have dreams. I think it is worth it. It is worth being committed to the Latin American reality, in an ecumenical atmosphere and an environment that is nurtured by Latin American liberation theology. I think that as young men and women theologians, we have a very big challenge in that the fathers and mothers of liberation theology are passing on or changing their theological focus. I take it as a challenge and I want to feed the dream that the youth will discover our role and contribution in this concrete reality.

Portraits! | Janet W. May, Editor

Janet W. May, Editor | Portraits

Coralia Blanco

Cuba, Baptist

My name is Teresa Blanco Coralia Elizalde. I work at the Martin Luther King, Jr. Center, in Cuba. I am a Baptist pastor. My job is coordinating the university-level study program and the diploma program in pastoral theology and social responsibility. The work is steady with students and people who are seeking a different kind of theological education. Also, I'm a pastor at a local church. I really would like for it to be a new kind of church where I can put into practice the knowledge gained through years of study at the Latin American Biblical University.

I didn't participate actively in the church until 1994 when there was an enormous growth in the number of people in the churches in Cuba. Since then, I had concerns and wanted to learn how to understand the Bible, so I enrolled in the pastoral education course CEPAS* at my local church. However, I did not want to be a theologian or a pastor, I did'nt understand any of that. The only thing I knew was that my church needed to strengthen its Christian education program and I wanted to prepare myself for that. I learned that in Cuba there was the Evangelical Seminary of Matanzas and my denomination, the Fraternity of Baptist Churches of Cuba, had relations with them and were sending students there. I wanted to study there, so I began to develop missionary work as a lay worker for my denomination. I opened a mission near my church; I live in Guanajay and the place where the mission was opened is called Callao.

*CEPAS is a program of the UBL.

Well, I continued but I was not baptized, and for the Baptists, baptism is very important. It was kind of funny, because several times I could not be baptized because there was no water, because the water was contaminated, or because the baptistry had not been filled. In the end I was baptized at a meeting of our denomination in 1994, a very cold day.

Finally, I delivered a letter to the Reverend Garcia, who was the secretary of theological studies at the time. Since I did not know what it meant to be a pastor or theologian, I said I wanted to develop my pastoral calling, using words from the CEPAS program that describes ministry. Time went by without a reply, because they said that I had to be more mature, but Raul Suarez, the director of the center where I work, knew of my work in Guanajay, he said what they were doing to me was an abuse but that I shouldn't worry, that agreements were being reached with the Latin American Biblical Seminary and that he would support my studies. I still did not understand what it meant to be a theologian and pastor, and I repeat that, because really what I wanted was to develop a ministry of Christian education.

One day in 1996, we were called and had an initial meeting. I became convinced that I wanted to be a theologian, that's where I began to learn what it meant to be a theologian. Of course, at that time I understood theology as a reflection on God acting in history. That struck me as fascinating because it was something I had never encountered outside of the CEPAS program and the books I had read. Then, in 1998, I was chosen to participate in the training workshop in sociological formation at the DEI*, because my work is part of the Martin Luther King Center. Talking to Pablo Richard and Mireya Baltodano, I learned that there were openings for scholarships at the UBL. So, I applied and advanced a lot in my studies. I began to understand that theology is not only the rational discussion about God, but that theology also passes through the body, through feelings, in human relationships that one builds and that give meaning to life. I was hooked on theology, but I still had a problem with being a pastor, because I felt like it was a position of power. I felt that the laity had more to say than the pastors.

Well, I left Cuba at the end of 1998 and returned there in 2000. In Costa Rica, I went to the Baptist Church and twice to the Episcopal Church. Then, Nidia Fonseca, who was in charge of the Pastoral Bible Institute, invited me to take charge of her church, because she was going to travel. She introduced me and everything was very nice. When the new building of the Costa Rican Wesleyan

---

The Departamento Ecuménico de Investigación (DEI) is an ecumenical research and training organization in San José, Costa Rica.

Methodist Church was beginning, we laid the first stone and then I realized that it did not matter being laity or a pastor if you were at the service of the church. You have to study to be of service to the church from a critical biblical, theological and pastoral perspective, and that is why I chose to study theology. Although the UBL breaks traditional patterns of education, it remains Latin American in its ways. Taking the image of the mountain from the Bible, when one goes up the mountain to learn, the true learning and challenge happens when you are in the community. I think that classes provide a lot but the important thing for me was that theology is not the responsibility of the theologian who studies it, but of the community in which that learning is put into practice.

When I am confronted with the situations of everyday life that go beyond intellectual questions, I do not have time to think about what I studied, what a professor said to me. However, theological studies provide a basis for choices, not just for you as a person but as a person in community. That is how the university has helped me. The university is one of the spaces for learning, not only in the classroom, but also in the student life, the student-teacher relationship, which is very different from traditional academic relationships. It's a great family. For me, personally, I do not want to be selfish by mentioning some and not others, but two professors have marked my life. One is no longer with us; he was Professor Arturo Piedra. He always told me that one was not a good teacher of theology or Bible if you didn't have a church to support you. It's not just about being a pastor, but being connected to pastoral work. The second person isn't second for being less important; he is Professor Roy May, who was the tutor for my thesis. He gave me a new vision into what ethics means, not only in terms of classes but also as a commitment. These are two professors who have influenced me. But it would be unfair not to mention Mortimer Arias, who was like a co-tutor for my thesis, and also many other women who have influenced my training. These people have developed their teaching ministries in connection with their pastoral commitment and their commitment to Latin America. They are not the only ones, but are the ones who have influenced me in my training and my life choices.

My dreams are very connected to my life and work. My greatest dream is to see my church formed. It's an irreverent church. I say this with pride; in fact, it has no pulpit and is a Baptist Church! Can you imagine a Baptist church without a pulpit, a church that what gives meaning to their social commitment and service, proclaiming and acting out their understanding of respect for life? Respect for life in all its dimensions. They are people who have had different theological formations and some are just are starting. Another of my great dreams is to see a Church, not a local church but a great church, a church with a capital C, to see it tied to everything that is the life experience of the human being, a church truly embodied in humans. This is where I see the mission of the Church.

Another dream stems from my work at the Martin Luther King Memorial Center. After ten years of working there, we're celebrating its twentieth anniversary. In my ten years of work, from 1995 to 2005, we saw that we already had served more than a thousand people. For me, it is a great satisfaction to see people committed to the churches and maintaining a level of critical thinking, not only about our church but also about society, not just Latin American and Cuban, but globally. I like to think it's a community that is embodied. My dream is to see religious pluralism flourish in a way that is something real, that when I participate in a service I remember my friend, my sister, who is talking to the Pachamama, the Orishas, Quetzalcoatl, to all our gods that form the pantheon of Latin America, that's my dream.

As for people who want to study theology, I don't want to be unfair, but I would like to ask first if he or she really has a pastoral vocation, if they are interested in being involved in the church, if they want to follow God and get their feet muddy in history. So, if they have their feet muddy in theological affairs, then they should study theology. If not, wait to be muddied, and then study theology. If they muddy their feet in ecclesial life and community, they would have my full support, because I believe that the person who has the intention and commitment at the church level will know whether it is worth studying theology or not.

Janet W. May, Editor | Portraits

Ángel Román

Guatemala, Episcopal

My name is Angel Eduardo Román Lopez, mestizo, of Guatemalan origin and living in Switzerland since 2004. Currently, I am working on a doctorate in practical theology at the University of Fribourg in Switzerland, with the subject of Youth dependent on addictive substances. The interest of this doctoral work is to provide theological and pastoral approaches to the Christian movements (especially Pentecostals) working the issue of rehabilitation of young people who have had contact with addictive substances, specifically with "crack". My pastoral experience has been primarily developed in the context of the Episcopal Church of Guatemala, accompanying and assisting in the processes of growth of youth groups. However, my experience in the theme of addictive substances has been ecumenical.

Deciding to study theology was nearly a 15 year process. When I was 20 years old, a soldier shot me in the chest, chipping my spine and I was left medically paraplegic, so I was expected to need a wheelchair for the rest of my life. I used it for just one month, afterwards using crutches and now, although I have difficulty walking, I do pretty well. After six months of struggling with suicidal thoughts from my state of denial of what happened to me, I started asking myself questions about the meaning of my life.

Then came the need in me to do something to not feel so "useless" as I had been feeling and I came to accept my new situation. Almost simultaneously, through my mom, I met a group of people from a church, which was Episcopal, who supported me a lot in making me feel useful and I joined the youth group and other church groups. Then I discovered that despite my physical limitations, I had other skills that could be used to feel useful. I discovered that I wanted to serve; I wanted to help other people like me who had difficulty integrating positively into their social context. And, curiously, I started working with young people dependent on addictive substances.

I studied chemical engineering, but ultimately decided I did not want to do that, but rather was eager to improve my pastoral practice. So, I entered the seminary of the Episcopal Church of Guatemala. Then I took courses through the distance program of the UBL in Guatemala, through CEDEPCA (Evangelical Center for Pastoral Studies in Central America), where I became interested in taking all the courses, especially those on gender and those related to the Latin American reality and with pastoral ministry. Then, I studied in Costa Rica at the UBL, where I finished my bachelor's degree, a licenciature degree and, finally, a master's degree in theology. During those years of study at the UBL I also managed my time, teaching classes in CEDEPCA.

It is very difficult to point to any single situation that highlights the importance or impact of theological studies in my ministry. I think it is easier to say that my practice is what motivated me to take up theological studies. By that, I mean that, in the beginning, I just wanted to be "useful" and began to work accompanying boys and men who consumed "crack". I was surprised to learn that they asked themselves questions about God, something that in my mind did not even exist as an alternative in my life. These guys who could not incorporate or integrate into society in a constructive manner had always hoped that one day "God would help them". Within their language there were always concepts and ideas about God. But, almost always their concepts and ideas about God were very fundamentalist. They felt sinful because they thought God did not want them or because they were evil by nature ("flesh is bad by nature"), their life was the result of "God's punishment", they always commented that "their soul was lost," and so on. At first, I didn't understand how they had such a "Christian" language. Then I realized that they only reproduced the theological language of the churches in the neighborhoods, especially the Pentecostals. That impacted me greatly, so I had to incorporate theology into my work.

Little by little, I discovered that it was easier to support a ministry of this kind by using the Bible and turning to a liberating reflection on it. But it was also necessary to use the Bible to talk with some pastors who were very influential in popular contexts, because it was impossible to ask them to support community projects in without drawing upon the Bible for support. But, when one has studied the Bible and has clear theological concepts, that task becomes easier. I realized that the more I knew about theology and the Bible, the easier it was to find support for our ministry and, of course, to open liberating spaces for youth dependent on addictive substances. In short, my practice impacted my desire to study theology and my theological studies afterwards impacted my practice.

An example of this was when I was in CEDEPCA, working as a teacher. I realized the importance of theological studies, not only for my pastoral practice, but for pastoral work in conjunction with different denominations. The strength of theological, biblical and pastoral knowledge acquired at the UBL helped me motivate leaders of different churches to incorporate liberating criteria into their theologies without forsaking their own identity.

I have dreams of completing my doctoral studies and returning to Latin America with my partner, Simone. My dream is not only mine, it is a dream shared with my partner. When I am finished with my studies, we plan to return to Latin America to work. My partner is also a Catholic theologian and works as a pastoral assistant to the church in the town where we live. But as dreams are dreams, we try to keep them flexible, to allow us to continue dreaming. So, she and I have the security that in some way God will show us the path.

Giving advice to people starting to study theology is the hardest part, because I cannot imagine giving advice. However, what I'm going to try to do is to make a suggestion. My view is that theology is not a profession, but a way to live and feel life. My suggestion is to view theological studies as a tool to improve pastoral practice and not as an end. That's why I consider that one does not have to study theology "to know what to do", but to know "how to improve what one already does". Well, I don't think that theological studies serves to make me happy, but rather serves to share with other people in a more effective way the joy that I already live.

Portraits! | Janet W. May, Editor

Larry Madrigal

El Salvador, Independent

I am Larry Jose Madrigal. I am Salvadoran. I work in the Bartolomé de las Casas Center in San Salvador. I accompany the general coordination and the Masculinities program in research, particularly on religious imagery. In addition, my pastoral experience is focused in two broad areas. One has to do with popular reading the Bible, with different groups in the rural areas and in the city. The other has to do with very specific workshops in which we evaluate the Biblical reading, and gender construction. Pastorally speaking, they are also part of my work but in different communities of faith throughout the country.

How did I decide to study theology? That is complicated to answer! You know that I am a son of the wartime period here in El Salvador, speaking generationally. I grew up in a base community in which there was a very strong understanding of the relationship between faith and the national political reality. I decided to study theology because I realized that many of the things that I looked for had answers in the theology that I heard preached at that time. But, also I realized that the theology that I listened to needed the contributions of younger people and laity, connected to the problems of daily living. Then, I began to look for a program that offered those things to me, but it was very difficult. I found contacts with a program in El Salvador in the Central American University, and I began to study there. But, soon I realized that was not what I was looking for. I needed something but contextual, but diverse, and also strongly directed to the specific problems that I was identifying. Some of my professors recommended a program to me in Costa Rica, at a place called the Latin American Biblical Seminary, because this program offered an ecumenical, Biblical perspective and seemed to also offer perspectives connected with some of the problems that I was identifying. Then I decided to leave the program in El Salvador and transfer to this other program that proved to be what I was looking for.

One of the best results of having studied theology is the ability to see reality from different perspectives, and from multiple perspectives. I believe that theology is able to recognize the contributions of a variety of disciplines and fields of knowledge, bringing them together in order to better understand the reality in which I work. This means that not only my experience is important, but also that of other people, such as in the ecumenical movement, the experiences of other racial and cultural groups, of different experiences of gender identity. Another example of the impact of theological studies is that faith transcends frontiers. The International study context allowed me to step out of my narrow, provincial experience and see reality differently. I think that studying theology has helped me to find a better sense of depth in what I do, a way of making sense of what I am doing, where I am going and why. These questions can't be answered just by consulting limited resources. I think that theology has helped me to seek not the official, doctrinally correct answers, but instead, to reflect profoundly on what it is that I am doing and what I am seeking.

One thing I am passionate about is, when conversing about feminista theology, I feel challenged and questioned. Like Roy* said some time back, I feel internal conflict, asking where is the image of God that as a male I am sensing, that I am discovering? This is a huge callenge, to think about God and divinity from a perspective of appreciation of categories that are new to me. It is troubling, because I have to undo things already learned and discover new, valuable and important things. Another challenge I confront is figuring out how to translate new ideas into ways of speaking that I can share with ordinary men, men with whom I work. At this juncture between religión and gender, what do I do? In a recent issue of Ribla, there was an article about Joseph in Egypt. OK, this is interesting research, but how do I share it with the men in the workshops? Every time I encounter new ideas, I am challenged with how to share them.

Regarding what I would say to somebody who was thinking of studying theology, one of the first things I would feel would be joy, because few people are interested in theology. I would want to know why he or she wants to study

*Roy H. May is a professor at the UBL.

theology. I say this because studying theology is not a way to escape from everyday reality nor is it a means of social or ecclesiastical ascent. On the contrary, studying theology causes problems, but it also brings great satisfaction, but not in a way that most people understand. It can even earn you enemies. So I would share these ideas, to see the reaction, and to see if the person really has a passion for theology at a moment when things are difficult and horizons are limited. But I would also say that the person is about to enter a fantastic new universe where he or she will find people from many contexts, and with many questions. There will be opportunities to appreciate the things you relieve and to think ideas that before you didn't dare to think. You enter a very privileged world where there will be opportunities for dialogue and for discovering many new things. It is difficult, but it is also fantastic. That's what I would say. I don't know if that would discourage somebody or not.

Portraits! | Janet W. May, Editor

Azucena López

Nicaragua, Church of God

I am Azucena Lopez; I am Nicaraguan. I participate in a Pentecostal church in Nicaragua, the Church of God. My parents have been in the ministry for almost thirty years, so I grew up in a pastoral family. My dad is nearing the end of his ministry and is currently supporting me much more, but physically he can no longer help.

I am currently working in the area of a project for women. The idea is to make it self-sustaining and for the moment we are taking some small steps. What we seek is that poor women can be productive by their own means, in order to sustain themselves, and that they have something to eat. They sew and produce crafts that we are selling. In Nicaragua there is a lot of unemployment, there are many single women with children, so it is very challenging.

The church also strongly supports education for teachers. As part of this, I work in the Baptist Theological Seminary. I have worked in theological education as a Program Coordinator since 1997 and I've taught the Bible, mainly in the Old Testament, since 1994.

Deciding to study theology was really a complete change in my life. I studied economics and worked in administrative accounting. I have a degree in Business Administration and Accounting. I worked in that field, but I felt a strong desire to study theology, especially because of my experience in the church teaching young people.

Portraits! | Janet W. May, Editor

Azucena López

Later, I was called to work at a national level in the church, in the area of Sunday schools and workshops. All of a sudden I was encountering questions that I could not answer. I said, "I need to study the Bible more; I have to study theology." I saw the need in our Pentecostal churches, that there wasn't a lot of training in theology or Bible and I knew that I could use my position at the national level to mobilize the churches in other areas. I saw that I could help and that is how I began to study theology.

Everything I have learned in my theological studies has been helpful to me because at the seminary I coordinate a training program. My administrative skills help me, but the field is very different. I worked with numbers in accounting; it seemed very cold. It is different to work in theology and with people because one learns to have relationships with people and discover their needs. One can learn from the experiences of many lives, and also grow, because it is not just about teaching but learning as well.

Theological study is important for me. Now I feel that I can contribute more to the people. For example, in our Pentecostal churches, I looked at the needs of the women, and had ideas but wasn't able to act on them. I couldn't do anything because I needed to learn more, but now, with everything that I've learned and especially the study of theology from the perspective of women, it has helped me to see myself in a different way, to improve my self-esteem, to reject some things that the churches teach about women. In reality it has been a process of de-constructing myself, and at the same time it has given me the strength to support and advance some ideas and projects with women with more confidence, because I know that I now have foundations that I previously didn't have. I had hunches and some ideas that I could not clarify. Over time, I've been learning a lot of things and I know that the place of women in the church is very different from what is preached.

This affects how I am writing my thesis. I'm working on Jesus and the Samaritan woman. The figure of the Samaritan woman has impacted me a lot because there I find that this woman had a very strong personality, secure, capable of making decisions by herself, without being intimidated by the canons that restricted women to certain areas. She is able to establish a one on one dialogue with Jesus.

One of my dreams is to be able to carry out the projects I've started at the seminary. I wish to support more training for women because there are already more men than women studying theology.

As for advice to people thinking of studying theology, I'd tell women that it can be very enriching. There is space outside the house. I've said to women many times that the house is a place for everyone, but there are also other spaces and other places. I would like to convince them to come to learn, motivate them and make them feel that there is a place for them; there is also a ministry for women from God. I'd invite them to be of service to the whole community, to be prepared to serve and de-construct all those models that are sometimes so strong.

Portraits! | Janet W. May, Editor

Elsa Tamez

Mexico and Costa Rica
Presbyterian and Metodist

I am Elsa Tamez. At this momento, I am a translation consultant for the United Bible Society. Before, I worked 25 years as a professor at the Latin American Biblical University. First, of course, it was a seminary and now it's a university. I studied in the seminary from 1969 to 1973 and I graduated with a Bachelor's degree in Theology in 1973. At that time, I returned to Mexico. Then, in 1976 I returned to Costa Rica for licenciature studies and I defended my thesis in 1979. When I came back in 1976, I also began to study at the National University for a Liecenciature in Literature and Linguistics, and I defended that thesis in 1985. I published my first books in 1978, one book and a Greek-Spanish dictionary. When I was back in Mexico in 1973, I worked for the United Bible Society and it was there that they asked me to do the dictionary. It was published in Germany in 1978 and is still the basic dictionary for New Testament that is published in Greek, and at the same time it is sold separately. The other book that I published in 1978 was titled *La hora de la vida* (The time of life). It was a Collection of biblical readings that was published by the DEI. Later, in 1979, I published a book that became well known and was translated into six different languages. It was titled *La Biblia de los oprimidos* (The Bible of the oppressed). It was my licenciature thesis for the Latin American Biblical Seminary. By that time, I was already teaching in the seminary. I had begun working at the DEI in 1977, as a student, and Hugo Assmann was the director.

Portraits! | Janet W. May, Editor
Elsa Tamez

When I began at the SBL, I taught Greek, Hebrew, Spanish, literature, and writing skills, all in the general studies program. Later I began to teach biblical courses. Sometimes I taught in Old Testament and then I did my doctorate in New Testament. That was from 1987 to 1990. I have been teaching and writing for nearly 30 years.

I decided to study theology because I was always involved with the church. I grew up in a very conservative church and I was always very spiritual. I wanted to be a missionary and work with Indigenous people. That was the idealismo that I had. I evangelized in the streets at times. It was very interesting. I wanted to study in a seminary but women weren't allowed. In the Presbyterian Seminary, women were only allowed to attend the Bible Institute, where it wasn't necessary to have a high school diploma to be accepted. But the men went to the seminary. In Costa Rica, women were allowed in the seminary. So, my brother Carlos asked me if I wanted to come study here because he was already an SBL student. I worked as a receptionist in a petroleum company and when he asked me if I wanted to come study theology I said yes, and I began studying here when I was 18 years old.

We were very poor and I had wanted to study chemisty, but my sister asked, "Who is going to pay for your studies? You have to study in a shorter program, like secretarial skills, and go to work." So, I studied typing and secretarial work and that's why I was working as a receptionist. But, of course, going to seminary drastically changed my theology, it shaped me and opened new horizons. At that time, Liberation Theology was very strong. I was in Germany in 1971, as an exchange student, and I took courses on the New Testament, social ethics and Hebrew. There were interesting things happening there and it opened horizons for me.

When I was in seminary, I discovered the biblical sciences and I felt very disappointed with what I had previously learned. This happened in Germany, too. What really helped me to respond, "Yes, this is what I want" was the discovery of Latin American contextual theology, a theology of liberation that responded to people's real needs, because back in the the '80's in Central America, there was a lot of repression going on in El Salvador, in Guatemala and right here in Costa Rica. Liberation theology responded to that reality. And, I came from a very poor family and one thing I can tell you is that when my mother died, I hated traditional theology that said that people who got sick were sinners. My mother laid in bed dying and asked, "What did I do wrong? I thought I was a good person." That hurt me so much, and that's why I responded to this new theology that was merciful, liberating, grace-filled and contextual. That's why I studied theology. Although I have given many lectures in important universities,

Janet W. May, Editor | Portraits

Elsa Tamez

the work I like best is working with ordinary people in biblical studies. I relieve that there is a real work of hope when people discover that God is different, especially for women. I really enjoy doing workshops with women; I have had incredible experiences when women discover that women are created in God's image. It is transforming, even physically, it changes completely their lives. For those of us who work in Feminist theology, this concept is so obvious, but at the grass-roots levels this is truly Good News for women.

After teaching 25 years at the UBL and after having served as the Rector for six years, now I am working with Indigenous people, as a translation consultant. I am helping Indigenous Colombians and people from other countries to translate the Old Testament. I have discovered another world that has been a source of great satisfaction. I also discovered the deaf community, a group that is marginated by hearing-able people. I studied sign language here in Costa Rica, because I was curious, from a linguistic perspective. I wanted to find out how ideas are expressed by bodily gestures. I have always enjoyed taking courses just for my own satisfaction. So, I studied sign language without realizing that this would open up a whole new area of ministry. Now, in my work, not only am I working with hearing people who are translating the Bible into their mother tongues, I am also serving as a consultant with a team of deaf translators who are translating the Bible into sign language from the perspective of the deaf community. So, I am very excited about this, and now I do more in workshops than in the academic classroom, even though in the university I teach one course a year and I work with thesis students. I don't want to give this up because it challenges me to stay up to date in my field. Last year, I gave a course on the gnostic texts. I had been wanting to study them and teaching always provides opportunities for research and learning. So, I am discovering every day more and more about the world of biblical translation and it is something I enjoy.

What would I say to somebody wanting to study theology? First, I would think, "Great!" and if it's a woman, we women theologians have worked very hard to stimulate women to study in this field, so I believe that it is very important for more women to study theology. But I also ask myself where they are going to find work, are the churches going to open their doors to women? I think Latin America is a religious continent, with many Roman Catholics and more and more evangelicals, and the dominant theology is extremely harmful to women. It is a literalist reading that privileges some texts and does not recognize the patriarcal cultures of the times in which the biblical texts were formed, today's patriarcal culture, the reader and the relationship between scripture and good news that is always liberating to people. This traditional theology is disastrous. Implicity, it can serve to legitimate the domestic violence that is a serious problem in Latin

America, and, above all, the assassination of women. So therefore I would say to to women, "Yes, study theology, but also study other disciplines. It has helped me enormously to relate theology to other fields. It has helped me in textual analysis that I also studied literature and linguistices, but there is also much to learn from anthropology and other fields that can nourish our research and enrich our theology.

Janet W. May, Editor | Portraits

Eduardo Chinchilla

Costa Rica, Methodist

My name is Eduardo Chinchilla. For the past four years I have been the regional secretary for the Latin American Council of Churches (CLAI) in Mesoamerica. It is a very wonderful ministry that God has given me the privilege to develop. I travel all seven countries from Mexico to Panama. This experience has broadened my horizon.

It is a ministry that the CLAI calls Pastoral Relationship. That is, I am the visible face of CLAI, closest to the churches in this region. It is a rich experience, to learn about the churches, to travel in rural areas, visiting the churches, preaching every weekend, being with young people, women, pastors, bishops and presidents and church leaders.

Regionally, the CLAI was not very well organized at the national levels. It is structured with delegates from each church. Each church appoints a delegate, whether it is a bishop, a pastor or a layperson. We work on plans to work together on a national issue, and we work as a region in common areas, like migration, free trade treaties, the culture of peace. I pay visits to churches in their assemblies, welcoming and supporting their ecumenical spirit. I have also been invited to be an observer for elections in several countries.

I have been in charge of CLAI's Culture of Peace program for the past two years. This program has taken up a challenge specific to El Salvador, Honduras, Guatemala and Nicaragua on the issue of gangs, called "maras". We help young people from churches and the churches themselves to reach out to these people, these young people, understanding their reality and encourage efforts

Portraits! | Janet W. May, Editor

Eduardo Chinchilla

in a culture of peace. There are churches that are helping youth to quit drug addiction. Many young people leave gangs, but there is only one reason they are permitted to leave and that is if they are going to a church. The maras are very well organized groups. It's gang warfare, but virtually the only way out is by going to a church. So this is a point in favor of the churches.

This work is very important because, for example, these boys have many tattoos when they leave. It is part of the gangs' form of expression. They are socially marked. There are churches that have programs to remove the tattoos, and this is something that we have encouraged. We have pushed forward dialogue between the police, the gangs and churches, and we have motivated and challenged governmental authorities and the police to respect the human rights of gang members or ex-gang members. The police forces that have taken the largest steps, including spiritual ones, are the Nicaraguan National Police and they are teaching other police officers in Central America.

We are building a network of mediators for family conflicts. The approach is to support the peaceful resolution of conflicts within the family. We know that this will help mitigate and banish domestic violence, because the current violent way in which we seek to resolve conflicts is what is destroying us. Thank God, we are motivating the churches, and holding training workshops.

In Colombia and Brazil there are initiatives of churches, with the campaign "Peace begins at home", to regain the home as a place of safety. The program has developed training materials for teachers of Christian schools and church schools on the culture of peace and how to teach teachers - teachers of mathematics, science, and social studies, on how to live and teach the theme of Culture of Peace within their subject, like creating a circle of peace, in other words, establishing a way of life in the schools that is closer the Culture of Peace. Well, that's what we are working on now.

I would say that in some ways the Latin American Biblical Seminary has influenced me ever since I was a child. First, my brother Edwin studied at the SBL, when I was ten or eleven years old. I would go to the seminary with Edwin, and his classmates from other countries caught my attention. I saw they were from other countries and living together. They were my friends: Michael Grey, Julian, Hector, and many others. I was like the group mascot, I went with them to play football (soccer) and everywhere else. At the time, I didn't realize what it would mean later.

I was always a church guy. Since I was born, my mom took me, and I always thank God, if anything I am grateful to God, that it is the faith that my mom taught me and that she wanted to give me, something very valuable. What is most precious to me, after my life, of course, is that she taught me to believe in the Lord Jesus. For me, the church was my world, my friends were there and I went to classes in the school but I stayed apart from some things. Instead of going to school activities, I went to church activities: Christmas, New Year's Eve, the day of friendship and Easter. Even after Sunday school, we would go to play football on Sunday afternoon and then run home to shower and be at church that night. There were two services, one in the morning and evening.

I was introduced to the world of the church in the level of leadership, thanks to pastors who stood by me and looked after me, like Jorge Enrique Rodriguez and Trino Flores who saw my potential as a leader. I started as the Sunday school secretary, then at church assemblies, I presented statistics on how many students had arrived, how many studied the Bible, that sort of things, then I was a Sunday school teacher, with small classes at the church. Then I was the Sunday school superintendent, and it was like that, little by little, from the first step.

When I was sixteen years old, I was about to graduate from high school. There was an evangelistic campaign in the church and Saturday night, the penultimate night, I felt a very strong call from the Lord Jesus, who told me that he had chosen to be his servant and called me to be a pastor. It was something very interesting, a very enriching experience that I could not ignore, so I went to the altar and told the guest preacher. I told him I felt God's call to serve and he prayed for me. At that time, Trino Flores was the pastor. I took some short courses and earned the rank of Local Preacher, that is to say that I was already part of the preaching team. Then God set in me the hope of studying theology. So I got out of school, at age seventeen. I didn't graduate from high school because I failed two mathematics tests. Finally, I passed the third one and came to the seminary, even though I had not formally received my diploma.

I remember Alicia Chacon said that I was the only student of the Latin American Biblical Seminary who had come to enroll accompanied by his mom. My mother took me to enroll at the seminary, just as she took me to enroll in elementary and secondary school. Well, I don't know, it fills me with pride and I say "good". That's as far as my mom took me, and that's fine, she is a great woman to me. I am very proud of that.

There were two problems: I could not be a regular student like others because, first, I was not yet 18 years old. On the other hand, I didn't have a high school diploma, which was a prerequisite for entering the Bachelor of Theology program. Dr. Mortimer Arias was the rector at that time. Alicia told me she thought I needed an interview with the rector, as is she didn't dare let me enroll, since I didn't have the pre-requisites.

Portraits! | Janet W. May, Editor

Eduardo Chinchilla

Mortimer received me in a very good way. We talked, conversed, and he asked me why I wanted to enter the seminary. I told him that I felt the Lord's call to serve as pastor and to preach his word. I was convinced that I had to prepare myself for that. When we finished the interview, he said: "I do not know, but there is something that tells me I have to let you enter the seminary." At that time there was a distance program. So, until I was old enough and got my diploma, I studied with the distance program, and did not lose that first year. After meeting the enrollment requirements, the distance courses were validated by the seminary and I enrolled with everyone else. So, I left school at the end of November and in March I was starting lessons in the Latin American Biblical Seminary. That is how I got into seminary.

I entered a world I did not know. I was greatly amazed by the world of the Bible. It really was the first time I plunged into what was biblical, theological and pastoral thought. I have never been very theological, I am more biblical and pastoral, I have always been passionate about those two areas, but unlike some people who sometimes went into the seminary and within six months or a year would say, "How is it possible for them to say that Moses didn't write the Exodus"? Some people felt their faith shattered, they had to put it in a bag and rebuild it. I didn't experience that, because in some ways my previous training had prepared me for that. But, yes, I expanded my knowledge about the Bible. I had teachers who were also very patient. They understood that in me there was a desire to understand the Bible.

It also opened my horizons with regard to the ecumenical relationship of the world. It's something we lack at times; to be formed with an ecumenical spirit, first I have to know who I am. When I went to the seminary I knew who I was, I knew what it was to be a Methodist, my roots at the national level, my historical roots, my roots of faith. I knew it well, and then I was prepared to get acquainted with a Baptist, a Pentecostal, a Presbyterian, or a Lutheran and not feel threatened. It opened my horizon to listening and understanding the wealth of others, of other denominations. I said, "Lord, you brought me to a place of privilege, where I can get close to another without any barriers, without any distinction and, above all, feel like I am God's people and not just a member of the church."

I learned everything that I have developed in my pastoral work. I did not give myself the pastoral task as such, but learned to use a set of tools, ideas, concepts, approaches, including processing, sensitivity to people, which is something I think is important. I reconfirmed my love for the people, because God called me to take care of his people. I loved the people, but later, as I took pastoral courses, I increasingly felt that people needed to be accompanied. I think it is very important that a pastor accompany his people in the search for green pastures, using the metaphor of the shepherd of sheep, who seeks that people always have fresh food, and that all is well, that life is full.

Another thing that was important in seminary was the liturgical growth. At the Seminario Bíblico I grew a lot liturgically. To me, it represented the best school of liturgy that I have had in my life and for me that was very important. I was part of the choir and many times my brother, Edwin, would join us. He joined the seminary after returning from Argentina and it made me glad because Edwin was the choir director at our childhood church. Back then, we always had our fights, because I was young, but I kept quiet because we had to rehearse. Once again, he got to direct the choir I was in at the seminary. The Lord doesn't have much mercy for Edwin, I think, because I'm back in a choir that he directs, but he's a very good director and always very motivating.

In pastoral work, there are many experiences where one applies what they have learned. I remember once, visiting a Nicaraguan immigrant woman in a community called Las Palmas in Guido de Desamparados, in a socially disadvantaged area. There's a lot of problems with drugs and crime. She had approached the church. She had two children, was pregnant and her husband beat her. Then I started to accompany her. I would walk with my Bible by a small creek; because of it her house was difficult to access. It was a tin hut, and on the way I encountered to four persons. They were selling drugs, Crack, and I was with my Bible. Then I said: 'Lord, well, what can I do"? I have to pass; and I did, I greeted them and it was interesting because one of them said to me: "Go on by, pastor, do not worry about anything". I had not gone to the house before. That was the first encounter I had before getting to where this woman was, that group of people, men who were there trafficking drugs.

I arrived and the outlook was very disappointing. I had to use everything I learned. It was an experience where I had to take out all the tools. I put myself in their place. They invited me in and I accepted their invitation. I felt it was God who told me He wanted me to be there. It was then that I understood Jesus who walked in the midst of the people and responded to the needs of the individual. I understood the Jesus of the Bible, Jesus as the theology of many books, the Lord Jesus which we celebrate every day. That was an event that marked my life because it was and remains a dangerous area in the community of Desamparados where I was pastor.

Working in the CLAI, I realized that God wants more than denominationalism. There is a need to realize that the Reign of God always transcends the Church; the Kingdom of God is not exclusive to the Church. The Church is a path in the

Portraits! | Janet W. May, Editor

Eduardo Chinchilla

Reign of God, but there are other paths. As I said in a sermon, in the Reign of God, God is the one that creates the roads so there is no way of getting lost.

I think it's time to move closer to the conservative churches and to Catholics, and to reserve our criticism. I think we need to agree to build together. I had some experience with conservative groups here in Costa Rica. There has even begun to be an inclusive opening towards the Catholic Church. I dream that one day we can sit down, as leaders of various Christian churches here in the country and pose a common agenda in favor of the country. On the other hand, all I want is that God fulfills His will in me, and once I told Him: "Lord, you can take everything from me, or life can take everything from me, or someone can take away everything, but do not let me lose the will to serve. I can lose everything but the will to serve" because that is what's most important to me, to serve God.

I think this is a time of challenge in Latin America. There have been many changes at the political level. It's important to know how to interpret them, approach with wisdom, in the name of God. There are no bells to ring, but there are economic and political projects that are being woven in the region. At the same time, we must be careful because not everything that glitters is gold, like the popular saying goes. We must have much more prudence to be able to interpret the signs of today's times.

As for advice for people thinking of studying theology, the first thing is to be very sure that God has called you. When you are sure that God has called you, everything goes forward. With that, I mean the pastoral vocation, because there will be some frustrations along the way. We must learn to say yes to God. That's how I did it and I do not regret it. It is perhaps one of the biggest steps I have taken in my life, to say yes to God. When I was called, it was like the prophet said: "Here I am, send me."

On the other hand, I think it is important to never stop loving people. It doesn't matter how many books one reads, or how many classes one takes, this training will be challenged in community with real people and sometimes the reality we see will say something other than what theory says. That's where we learn to combine theory with practice, to discern.

We must always walk with the vision of the church as a healing community. We must develop ministries in this regard. In our world there are people who are suffering a lot, for many reasons. The church has to be a therapeutic place where people grow in their lives. We have to learn to laugh with people, to mourn with the people, to walk with people in a downpour without an umbrella, including foregoing a bite of food to give it to others. Well, these are the tips that I would give those who wish to study theology.

Another thing I would like to emphasize is that I have reached the conviction that the pastor should no longer be an adviser. Perhaps some will think of this as heresy. I think we should be mediators, because what I have realized is that advising brings us problems, because people come and want us to solve the problem for them, and it's a feeling of power to pretend to know everything. As a mediator, the pastor teaches people that the answer lies in them, and that the problem is theirs and not the pastor's. I believe that the high blood pressure, back pain, and other chronic diseases which many pastors suffer is because we have taken the problems of others onto ourselves. We want to resolve the problems, but we can't, because in the end they can't be resolved. Psychologically, every person is the source of his or her own answer. What we can do is to orient people on how to resolve conflicts, whether they are internal, family or work related, wherever the problem is. It is necessary to help seek a peaceful and edifying solution for all, and in that sense being a mediator rather than counselor.

Well, these are my suggestions, as a pastor who came to study theology accompanied by his mother and what I have learned from these studies.

Portraits! | Janet W. May, Editor

Eduardo Chinchilla

Janet W. May, Editor | Portraits

Marlen Dell

Costa Rica, Baptist

My name is Marlen Dell. I am Costa Rican and I direct the Caribbean Theological Center in Limón. I am also the pastor of the First Baptist Church of Limón, which in reality is the first Baptist Church in Costa Rica. I did this work for many years without being recognized as the pastor. Historically, I worked with the missionaries that came here and when they weren't here, I was in charge of the church, of the diaconate, of everything, but it wasn't until 1998 that I was asked to take on the responsibility of pastor.

Studying theology is something I felt called in my heart to do when I was 16 years old. But at that time I thought for certain that something was wrong with me, because that wasn't something women were involved in. Back then I wanted to enter the Latin American Biblical Seminary, but, when I finished high school, I opted to go to the university: I was going to study physics and mathematics, but I ended up studying primary education. Parallel to this, I read anything I could get my hands on about the Bible, about my dreams, because I thought that I was called to be a missionary in some part of the world. So I read a lot of books about the Bible, commentaries, and Biblical dictionaries in order to clarify concepts and then later, before becoming a pastor but working with missionaries, in 1986 we began to talk about creating a leadership training program. At that time, we didn't have any pastors. I was helping a circuit of five churches. So, we decided to open the Caribbean Theological Center in 1993 or 1994. For the first time, I took a course in the Latin American Biblical Seminary. It was about leadership alternatives. This was a very emotional moment for me because, as you see, it was the fulfillment of the call I had had many years earlier. This was the first course I took and later I began taking theological extension courses in Limón, through the Caribbean Theological Center. I later finished the course work for a master's in theology from the Latin American Biblical University, but I still have to do the thesis.

I was helped a lot by the arrival of Ricardo Mayol and Doris Garcia, who came to Limón as missionaries of the American Baptist Chruch. They came to work with the Theological Center. This was important for me because I found a theological vision I could easily accommodate. Then, as I studied theology I found in the Bible answers to questions I had had since childhood, for example, different ways men and women are treated and similar things. Well, thank God my wise mom didn't make much of such differences. To begin studying theology was like putting on big eyeglasses that helped me find in the Bible and the life of Jesus answers to these questions that had always bothered me.

In my pastoral practice, I have been helped a lot by Christology and ecclesiology to understand what the church is. I believe that these are two bastions of pastoral work. But although they help, they also cause conflicts and difficulties, because at times the community doesn't understand the concept of church. They still think in pastor-centered terms, and want a pastor that is very directive, who puts everyone in their place. I see the church as an active organism in which every one has a part in its different functions, but of equal importance to the body. At times my pastoral practice helps me lead the church toward an understanding of Jesus's practice with his disciples. The church today has the responsibility of living inside the community, the local community, and feeling community realties and participating in generating answers, not to shut itself in a bubble and separate itself from the world. I believe theology is important for that, in order to have clarity of how the church ought to make Christ present now, in midst of our times.

Here in Limón we had some very beautiful experiences in the Caribbean Theological Community. At first the Center functioned in the church building, in 1995, at the time of the liberalization of the Limón Port Authority. What happened was terrible, it was a social debacle for the dock workers, so much so that people committed suicide. There were families that split up because the change was from one day to the next. We tried to make the church see that it was our responsibility to accompany these dock workers and it was hard for some in the church to understand that. But there were some good results. Richard and Doris had been here a couple of months and they had begun to preach but some evangelized dock workers also came around, and they had been evangelized in a different way. Because the church was accompanying them in all this they wanted to know why the church was doing this, because Ricardo was paying to have some platforms built that were going to be used in a demonstration by the dock workers. We took advantage of this opportunity to explain to them and then they understood. Now some of them are serving some churches and others seem to have lost their bearings, but they all lived this experience. Last week, there was a parade in Limón against violence and the church participated. From my church, a lot of youth and professionals were there, but also some retired women. The youth made the placards and the ladies carried them in the parade. In many cases, I have had the opportunity to help them see the church's role as important for the community. We are not here to have merry worship services; that is part, but not all. Rather, the church is present in the life of the community every day of the week, every hour of the day. We meet sometimes to recharge batteries, but the ministry of the church is done outside, in the community.

My personal dream, well, yesterday there was a ladies retreat, and I had told them that I would be there but not until mid-day. We went to a house in the countryside and I shared with them the passage where an angel says to Abraham that he is going to have a son with Sarah. But before sharing this passage, I told them to share their own dreams with each other and then with the group, and almost all the dreams had to do with children and grandchildren. Then, I called their attention to Sarah's attitude when the angel announced that she would have a son and that within a year she would be enjoying him, and she said, "How is this possible at my age to have pleasure?" I said to the women that this is the problem, that we feel that after menopause nothing is left, no dreams or projects, no goals, no visions. I shared with them that my dream is to finish the masters thesis; that is my personal dream.

Regarding the church, I have the dream of seeing the church more alive, more committed to the community. We have some activities now that before we didn't have. For example, every fifteen days we prepare lunches for everyone who wants to come, for those in the street, drug addicts and everyone else. At first the meals were prepared and they came and were served on throw-away plates. One day I told them that if we were going to do something, we should do it well. If we are going to give them food, well, it's not enough just to give them a plate outside. Let's set up tables! We have space. So every fifteen days a group of men and women church members come to cook, others bring something prepared at home, they set up tables, and people come and sit down to eat. Sometimes there are more than a hundred. They are given food and we share a meditation. I have made it clear to the church that we don't have to condition their coming to eat with accepting Jesus and coming to church, but that we do this because it is what we ought to do. We also pass out things they need. People come and prepare bags with essential items; we have a list of some one hundred people for the bags.

Apart from this dream, I also have another one. On the property next to the church there used to be a brothel. Drugs and everything were sold there. Last January, I told the church that we should buy the property and transform it into a place of blessing for the town. A year and a half ago, the police closed the place. Now it's there without being used, but I haven't convinced the church to buy it. They say we have a lot of space, that we don't need it, but I see a three-story building, with a good meeting hall, with offices, and that the Lord has given the church a lot of professionals who are willing to give their services to the needy. We have teachers, doctors, everything. I'm still waiting on this dream. We don't even need a loan. We have enough money in the bank right now, but I don't want to twist the arm of the church, I'm giving them an opportunity. I believe that if it is God's will that we buy the place, in time we'll buy it, because if we have money it's better to invest it in property than to leave it in the bank. We need to know how to use the financial blessing we have received.

My advice to people who want to study theology is "Go ahead!" Theology clears one's vision. One sees God differently than before, sees the world differently. There is a song that says, "Nothing is true, nothing is a lie, all is crystal clear." Theology is like seeing through a crystal, the Bible says we all see as if in a mirror, not clearly, so we see only a part of the whole, but with theology we begin to see more clearly. So, my recommendation is that many young people study theology. This is a problem for the church, we have lots of professionals but no one is thinking of studying theology. I especially encourage youth to study theology. If I had begun after leaving high school, perhaps I could have done other things, but I am happy that it's not too late. I encourage men and women to study theology so that they are able to unite with Jesus's project to preach and practice the Reign of God, and theology helps one do that.

Nidia Fonseca

Venezuela and Costa Rica
Pentecostal y Methodist

My name is Nidia Fonseca and I am Costa Rican. At this time I am working for the Latin American Biblical University. I am the Vice-rector, but the largest part of my work in the UBL has been non-university education, both for Costa Rica the rest of the continent. It is organized as the Pastoral Bible Institute. It also includes the Indigenous Program.

As for my pastoral experience, I think it's a pretty extensive. I think I was about nine years old when I discovered that my call was to serve others from the very specific perspective of the practice of Christian faith. I was going through a critical moment in life and was thinking about what shall I do? What will be my life? Where am I going to go? What quality of life I do I want to have? And what quality of person do I want to be? When I asked myself these questions, being so young, the first thing that came to mind was that I cannot answer these questions if I'm not clinging to something greater than me. That was when I started to develop my full commitment and faith, perhaps childish, but in God.

Then, at the age of twelve, a cousin gave me the challenge of participating in a Catholic group of teenagers and I accepted. I thought I could give some input from my experience because I was twelve years old. I had already participated as a teacher in Sunday school. So I thought I could make some contribution in that regard. As a teacher, I worked with eight, nine and ten year old kids.

Portraits! | Janet W. May, Editor

Nidia Fonseca

It was very nice because I found that it was a very large group. First, there were preteens, twelve year olds like me, and even guys who were in college, most of them Catholic. But there were others who were not Catholic and I was deeply struck by that. I found that the group was led by a Franciscan and two other Catholic priests. I remember at that time there was a great deal of influence and excitement by everything that had happened in Puebla.

That helped my ecumenical attitudes, because I was between the two waters. When I was a little older, perhaps sixteen years old, in the group movement, we started to ask a series of questions. We always began with personal stuff, and the traditional things that we experience as adolescents, like generational conflict with parents and all that. We discovered that if we all had similar conflicts it was because there was something beyond our family that was affecting society as a whole. Then one of the college students started telling us that it was an ideological matter, and we asked the priests if that was the case. Indeed, the Franciscan said, "Yes, it's an ideological matter." So, we started to analyze the society more broadly. He also studied sociology, so he could elaborate a little more. It was enough that we started to say, "if this is the society and this is happening in the family, then something must be happening in the church as well."

The movement was so large that it began to organize itself in various activities. We had several groups: a choir, a theater group, a cultural group, and folk dancing. We had a sports group and I participated in everything - in basketball, in relay races, in folk dancing and everything. So, for Easter, the musicians decided we were going to sing only music made by the group, and was very nice. But, of course, it reflected part of our concerns. There was a huge procession as part of this Holy Week. We were identified as the group from San Cayetano and even the Archbishop of San José came out. We realized they were going to reprimand the priests for having five or six of us in this movement that were not Catholics. The priests allowed us not only to participate but also to read the Bible and other things. We had been allowed to interpret the text, because they said we had more experience in that.

It was terrible. I do not know who told the monsignor what was being done, but they closed the church and put boards on the doors and windows. We went to remove the boards from the church because what we were doing was something we felt was very important. However, we had no awareness of how much we were really doing. Then I began to speak in my evangelical church about what we were doing, and there was also a problem. In the Methodist Church, they were afraid that I supposedly would be absorbed into Catholicism. This caused me many concerns. I realized that, little by little, the missionary pastor who was guiding me was very broad-minded, but at the same time, his concern was that I was to work more in line with the church and not according to society.

After the monsignor closed the Catholic Church, the group pulled the boards off the doors and windows. We had requested an opportunity to meet directly with the monsignor and he was ready to receive us. It was a very big movement and we had just formed a national youth movement that was being organized. We appealed to the youth movement, to all the youth groups from the Catholic Church. The monsignor decided to negotiate when he realized that the treasury of the national movement had joined us. He was very humble and agreed to go to the church to talk with us. We insisted that the three priests who supported the group be allowed to attend as observers. He accepted, but to them, later, the cost was very high, because they took the three priests out of the movement and sent them to seminaries, allegedly to train new seminarians. But the movement was already very big.

During the same years, I had participated in the ALCOHA movement, the first major student movement in Costa Rica against transnationals. I was very involved in the student movement from school, very active in two churches ministering in the perspective of liberation theology, and in the Methodist Church we were working with materials from CELADEC, New life in Christ.

I began to wonder what I wanted to study in college. At the same time, two new pastors arrived at the Methodist Church of Hatillo, a Costa Rican, and a Peruvian. The two were studying here at the Latin American Biblical Seminary. Then, there was an interview on Radio Universidad with Dr. Rodolfo Cerdas, who at that time was the director of the School of Political Sciences. When he explained what Political Science was, I said, "That's what I want to study, because there is my ministry." When I said that to both the priests and pastors, the only one who supported me was pastor Saul Trinidad* who was doing supervised ministry in the church of Hatillo. He invited me to think about the church as an institution, and where I was going to locate myself. Also, one of the priests told me that he thought it was excellent, but he seemed to think that I was too young to think about studying political science, but that it was very good that I wanted to develop my training, being a woman.

Until that moment, I did not see myself as different from others, when he said, "being a woman", I immediately thought of all the women in my family,

---

Saúl Trinidad was a student and later a professor of the SBL.

and it seemed very interesting, because of my dad's family, all my aunts and great-aunts are single professionals. And on my mom's side, all the women are housewives and married. Then, I began to sense that something was happening, that there were options that one could take and or choose to sacrifice. In addition, on a personal level, I did not see it as a very attractive choice to marry and be a housewife. I was more attracted to the other side, my aunts and great-aunts on my father's side. They were all teachers. I saw that, although they remained unmarried, they were happy, fulfilled, open. So I thought about things like that.

At the end of the fourth year of high school, I began to tell the priests that I was leaving the movement, because I wanted to have a deeper experience with the youth of the Methodist Church, to see what I wanted and where I was going. They not only encouraged me to do so but I was also told me that the doors were always open if I needed to come back and visit. I went to my church very pleased and happy to be involved with the youth group and I almost fainted when I saw what they were doing. They did one thing in Sunday school with CELADEC and something very different with the youth group. In other words, it was like the youth groups were playing house. So I told them that this could not be, and I started thinking about what we did in the Catholic group. They tried to put me into the board of directors for the youth group, but I preferred to accompany them in another way, as I did with the group in the Catholic Church. Then the missionary pastor, who was responsible for the church said to me, "You are going to start a ministry with these young people." It was very interesting, but it was extremely difficult for me because the Catholic group was very free, there were no problems of moral doctrine. By contrast, in the evangelical church, everything was reduced to a narrow moralism. Then Saul Trinidad, in the annual assembly, was appointed as pastor to my church. He felt more secure and called me to join the Christian Education team. That was when I had direct contact with the Seminario Biblico. I asked him what I had to do to enroll and the bandit and told me I had to have a university degree, even though that wasn't true. So, first I studied political sciences in hopes that, when it was completed, I would be able to enter the seminary. With Saul, we worked on the social engagement of the church in a more profound way. He began to invite me to the seminary at times, when there interesting activities. Then I met Victorio Araya*, after Saul suggested that he read a paper that I was going to present in a history course. I met Plutarco Bonilla* at the first assembly of the Methodist Evangelical Church that I attended, and I also met Elsa Tamez* and Jose Duque*. This was my second

---

* *Victorio Araya, Elsa Tamez and José Duque are all graduates of the SBL and are now professors at the UBL. Plutarco Bonilla is a former rector and professor of the the UBL.*

year at the university and I started to work harder in order to support my family. I began to work in Social Security.

From there on, my concerns were even greater. I learned that the pastoral ministry was not simply reduced to a church. I took the words of John Wesley, "the world is my parish" and I always had that phrase on my desk. I said, "My work is my parish, every where I am is my parish." Then I started to be concerned about my human relationships, working relations. My superiors had noticed that I had a different way of relating with peers and colleagues. When I was in the first semester of Political Science, my boss invited me to join the discussions in the department of public relations. I attended the discussions on publicity campaigns, but before that, when I began working there, I was invited to work in human relations and I started to raise some concerns similar to what I saw at the seminary, in terms of human relations, as it was really different from what I was seeing in the workplace. Also, I did some tests and I was told that my voice would be good for work as a radio announcer. So I enrolled in a program to study this and started working with the radio. I did not understand why this was a scandal for journalists, but soon after I realized I was the only female voice in all the radio stations of the country.

All this led me to feel more confident as to what I wanted in my ministry. This helped me to negotiate with the church for what I wanted to do. That was when I asked to be elected superintendent of the Sunday school and to be secretary of the local assembly. I began to realize that if I did not open my own spaces, they would never open. But the difference was in quality because I was thinking about social issues, concerns about society that I had at the time. I asked, for example, why can't we do something ourselves? Saul thought it was excellent and we formed a team to start doing community ministies.

I also saw my place of work as my parish, I began to take leadership regarding labor issues. When there was a problem, people would call me to see if there were other ways they could communicate what they wanted to say. I began to realize that the alleged problems were only with women. I was called very few times to deal with men. I noted that at least 70 percent of my male colleagues were alcoholics and would behave ridiculously every time there was a party. I was very worried about this and I immediately thought about their families because my dad was an alcoholic and I knew how it affected us. So I wondered how it affected my colleague's families. My boss also had those concerns. He asked me once, "Nidia what can we do?" Then I told him, "We have to do something. I took a copy of a devotional book called Desert Springs to the office and told my boss I wanted us to start having a moment of reflection, to hear what was happening in people's lives, because they were drinking for a reason. Today I can understand the whole issue of masculinity, but at that moment I felt that it was more of a subjective issue than an objective issue. So we started. A beautiful relationship developed between everyone and we became like one big family. There, one could discuss anything freely. It was a fellow group member who broke the ice, and began to talk about his personal situation. It was a place where I felt that the world was my parish.

Simultaneously, in college, I was met with tremendous challenges in political science, where everything was atheist. I said that I would not deny my faith. I took Victorio's book, *God of the poor: The mystery of God in Latin American Liberation Theology*. I began to reflect on all the work from the perspective of John Wesley.

In the Caja I had a number of leadership experiences. There was a woman on the board and she called me and another woman. We were greatly encouraged to continue in an administrative career in social security. The administrative career was not very attractive to me, so I said no, I want to be recognized as a political expert when I finished. So she told me: "Look, I am concerned because I have the feeling that here women only advance if they are entangled with the boss. If they aren't, then they don't advance. I've been reviewing this, and the only people who supposedly pass the administrative career exams are men and that can't be." So, I started to go by all the floors at noon, to see what women were on each floor and took note of their the names and positions. Then I took the list to Ms. Irma Morales. I said, "Here is my list of all the women and all the posts they occupy and you are right. They are all secretaries or receptionists but are studying other things." Then, she said, "Let's have a women's meeting." I made a flyer, calling for a meeting on a Saturday after noon. I wandered from office to office delivering the flyers to women, without saying anything. There were very few women who went to that meeting.

I remember Ms. Irma's famous question "How have you maintained this position?" Some said that the boss liked them a lot, and others felt very indignant. One cried a lot and said she had to give in to things she didn't want. I got scared, because they all said things like "You're lucky with your boss, all of us would have loved to be there in public relations, because there isn't any danger." I did not understand this because my colleagues were very respectful, too. So I went to two of my women colleagues, the oldest ones and I asked what they meant. One of them laughed and told me, "Look, I'm going to tell you what happens", and she began to tell me of the well-known "favors" for the bosses. I was very indignant. I said, "We have to do something, Ms. Irma." She had a lot more awareness. It took her a lot to get where she was and I do not know what personal experiences. But she told me, "I don't dare, I am afraid."

So I came to the seminary and spoke in a gathering about what was going on. Irene* and Elsa* were surprised that we had dared to organize that meeting, and that any woman would have dared to talk about what was going on. I started to hear some concerns from Irene, Elsa, and Raquel Rodriguez on the importance of reading the Bible from the perspective of women.

I had begun to study at the seminary. I had a very deep relationship with the Latin American leadership at the seminary. It helped me with many things; I also helped, like when they opened a public relations office. They asked me to advise the office because I already knew a lot about that.

At the seminary, like elsewhere, there was much concern. The seminary was deeply committed to the option for the poor. Even within the church, the president of the youth group in Honduras was "disappeared", two of the youths from the National Youth Board of the Methodist Church went to the armed struggle in Nicaragua. One of them disappeared and the other two returned well, but it shook the church. There was a meeting at the seminary and I listened to Raquel and Irene who said, "It is strategic for women who feel called to serve in the church to ask ourselves what kind of call we are experiencing and that we begin to differentiate between the call to service and the call for ordination in pastoral ministry." I thought things over and decided to seek ordination. So, I participated in the assemblies, I became a member of the National Department of Education, was the director of a Youth Camp for three consecutive years and in the fourth year I was named chaplain. It was all very interesting but I wasn't accepted for ordination. The pastors said that it was not because I was female. At that time we were Yolanda Bertosi, Mardi Vela and I all here at the seminary. Yolanda was an assistant to the course of Christian education; Mardi was well advanced and had even gone on a student exchange. As student who lived at home and work, my studies were going very slowly. I was only allowed to take one course per semester because I was working full time. I saw many groups graduate, because I could not carry more than two courses per year and because of my work, I could only study at night. I thank both José Duque and Luis Segreda* who were always sensitive to working students who could not study during the day. Duque invited me to participate when the DEI was being formed and the DEI started seminars on denominational traditions and theologies. I participated in the Methodist one and met lots of people, like Hugo Assmann and many others.

Irene Foulkes was a professor at the SBL and at the UBL. Elsa Tamez is a graduate of the SBL and professor of the UBL. Jose Duque and Luis Segreda are both graduates of the SBL. Luis Segreda was a professor and director of the library at the SBL. Jose Duque is a UBL professor.

Portraits! | Janet W. May, Editor

Nidia Fonseca

Then, I decided once again to ask the church to recognize me as a candidate for ministry, and it turned out to be a terrible ordeal. It was just two years after the Methodist Church had decided to renounce its relationship with the seminary as a place for preparation of their candidates and I remembered that Saul had warned me that I was going to get burnt, saying things like, "You're crazy, how dare you!" I said to him I am not going to study anywhere else other than here. I did something considered very shocking. I sent a letter to the chairman of the Committee on Ordained ministry and he said to me, "You're not a member of any Methodist Church." I almost died, I said "How is it that I am not a member of the Church in Hatillo?" He said, "No, your name is not in the books." I went to talk with a pastor and he said "No, your name isn't here." I said, "Yes, I am a member and I remember when I did the whole membership ceremony, with pastor Marion Woods. I remember that I signed a book." But the pastor said, "Your name is not here." But I saw that the book was missing a page, that there was a page torn from the book. And I said "a page missing here." I went to look for Marion Woods who was interned in the Clinica Biblica. I told his wife what was going on and she said to me "I speak because I know that you are a member. I don't understand why are you set on being in that place of studies, but you are a member." When Marion recovered he also said that I was a member and they said no, and I had to go back again to straighten things out and I was told that I couldn't do that in the church of Hatillo. That is when the doors to the church in San Sebastian were opened to me. I started everything all over again, but it was funny this time, because the pastor proceeded with the membership ceremony after six months. At the local assembly, I was named superintendent of Sunday school and director of youth and the following year restarted the process for ordination. With that, I was told that I had to wait two more years to be a candidate to the ministry again. It was during that time that I fell in love, got married, and moved to Venezuela.

In Venezuela I found a different church, a Pentecostal church that was very committed to social work. There I could unite social work with women within the church, and also in the people's movement. It opened my way into other places inside and outside the church. Then, upon returning to Costa Rica, I wanted to do different work in the church.

I left in 1985 and returned in 1992. I found an autonomous Methodist church that I have worked with ever since, a new denomination that had formed after I went to Venezuela. When it was my turn to take charge of a local church, I suggested that my concerns were twofold: to have a house where we could meet, and that I was not going to worry if the church had or didn't have members but instead that those I would guide would be Christians in the world, and not just within four walls. For example, a member of my church had spent ten years without going anywhere, almost fifteen years without leaving the house, or getting on a bus. She is now studying theology, is in social movements, and works as a volunteer in her community. To me this is a very important witness.

I think that if I had not studied theology and had not known the teachers and students that I knew, I would have possibly only worked in social movements. It was thanks to their testimony and opportunities for reflecting on them, that I could make the connection between church and society. This is why I proposed a pilot plan here at the UBL, so that Costa Rican women and other women living in Costa Rica could study theology. I proposed that it be with women, no matter their age, who never had a chance to gain access to theological reflection and to mature in their faith. That has been one of my contributions in the university that I feel very good about. I knew that, of those who could enter, perhaps 25% could stay, and that was just about right. We can say that at this moment that 35% of those who have entered are still here, and I'm sure they will finish. I want this program and its results to be evaluated so that I can ask the university to make it permanent, because the experiences of these women demonstrate significant changes.

I believe that what the seminary gave me could not be found in any other seminary. I had friends in the church who studied in other seminaries and today aren't doing anything. There are only two left, and only one in the Evangelical Methodist Church of Costa Rica. So, it's not just about studying theology, it's where you study theology and what theology is studied. So, if I meet people who want to serve and who want to give from their practice of faith, I recommend that they study theology, but not just anywhere.

I think that the UBL can do a lot more in Costa Rica than it has. There is much that we can develop, not only in formal education, nor the university program, but also in many other fields. Our ecological perspective, our vision of the pastoral accompaniment, and our ethical perspective can open other areas of service and reflection. That's one of my dreams, to open other spaces. I think that those spaces would not be limited to Costa Rica. I think we have to develop other types of networks and connections to do this. That's one of my dreams in the Vice-Rector's Office.

Another of dreams as Vice-Rector is that the administration could really give other types of support to the university. I think there are people for whom we have not opened spaces to awaken and grow their gifts in service. Although some have many years of work in the university, there is still a limit, a lack of openness to receive their input.

It doesn't hurt to have big dreams. I also believe that the university is going through very good and interesting challenges in the financial aspect, at the level of what we want to accomplish in Latin America, and in the quality of theological reflection and social transformation. I think the university, along with a network of Latin American institutions, has dreamed of a transformed society, but not necessarily passing through the body of the institutional Church. I think the challenge now is how to work towards making this vision a more concrete reality.

For those who want to study, I recommend they study here or in the network of theological institutions that approach theology in a contextual way. I recommend that they have the humility to be tolerant and to be open to diversity. That is our strength. You have to remain open, willing to learn and be tolerant of diversity, but with patience and humility.

Janet W. May, Editor | Portraits

Dorotea Yucra

Peru and Costa Rica, Independent

My name is Dorotea Yucra Cataño. At the moment I am working in the Christian Community Church, in Los Guidos sector 5. We are working with young people. I value young people because they are the hope of both the church and community. The Christian Community is a free church. Before, we were part of the FIEC, but we became independent around 1999 or 2000. Our commitment is deep, that people get to know God. This is not just about preaching and singing in the church. That is a part, but to know God, Jesus, we should invite all the people, women, and children, to other ministries. For example, we have had a meal program for many years for women and children. Our Gallo Pinto, a local Costa rican dish, is shared in the presence of the Lord. All the children sing "Lord bless our bread." So our main activity is to come closer to the people through their needs.

I have not led great evangelistic campaigns. I know these campaigns, I participated in these in Peru when I was a pastor there, but the result is minimal. Here, we are approaching through friendship. In that sense, we gained ground for evangelization. My work has been fruitful in approaching single women, foreign women, mostly Nicaraguans. They suffer for being foreign and poor. They have don't have goals because they are stranded by their situation, crushed by poverty and abandonment by husbands and neglected by the authorities in the church itself. Many people know foreigners but when they invite them into the church, the first thing they say to them is they have to to give money, they

Portraits! | Janet W. May, Editor
Dorotea Yucra

have to tithe. Women are afraid because they do not have a penny to give. They are working and may receive a pension, but the work they get is not enough; they do ironing and washing, for example. What they get is little money, to buy a little bit of food for their children. When I visit the women, I approach them with bread in hand, with coffee. I have coffee with them in their homes. They know me as the "bread woman," the woman who brings bread and coffee. The children are happy, because they know I'm coming with bread, coffee and milk to share. In this way, the women are learning to come closer and see the presence of God, that God walks with them, that God walks with the children. This has been my ministry in Los Guidos for three years.

At the beginning, my pastoral work was very difficult. We know how difficult it is to be accepted into the ministry as a woman, in an abandoned neighborhood, a shantytown, where there are no sidewalks to walk on. I am a foreign woman who came with her children and without a husband.

Before arriving in Costa Rica, I was in my own country, Peru. As a child I was a pastor, but of goats and sheep and I never let a fox get a lamb. Whenever one went missing, I would look for it, because there was almost always someone on the path who would save it, taking care of it until I arrived, and the reunion was always a great joy. Only once, a giant wolf captured a lamb. I carried a stick and the wolf was ahead of me dragging the sheep. I got it freed, it but when I came home with the lamb, my mom gave me a beating. Then I thought about how Christ suffered for the lambs.

I went from the mountains to Lima because of my husband's health, because everything is concentrated there, doctors and all the hospitals. We had nowhere to live, nothing to eat, and I did whatever work I could get. Soon, I was widowed, with my three children, jobless and without my husband's pension, taking almost two years for it to be processed. I went to church to pray, asking the Lord, and cried. In one of those times, I heard the invitation of the pastor to participate in pastoral studies. He said it was for the young, for men, but I wondered, a woman couldn't go? So I said, "Pastor, I can take that invitation." He replied, "No, you are a widow and a mother. These studies are for young people, for men. How old are you" "I am 37 years old," I said and he responded "You are supposed to stay at home." I said to him "What?" and he tells me, "Jesus said so, it says so in the Bible, and I have not seen where it says a woman may study to be pastor. And even a baptized woman cannot perform the Holy Communion liturgy."

I insisted and signed up for the SBL's Prodiadis program. To pay for the study materials and books, I sold food on the street. But the books and materials never arrived. I wrote to the SBL, complaining, and they re-sent them, but they never came. One day, a lady at the church told me that the materials had arrived but the pastor was hiding them. I went and confronted him. I got my materials and after that I asked the SBL to send the materials to another address.

At the beginning, I was not accepted in the pastoral ministry. Everybody wanted me to go home. They were embarrassed to be guided by a woman and objected to all aspects of my body. Everything was wrong, mostly because I cut my hair and wore trousers. Even children complained. They asked me "Why do you wear pants?" Then, a twelve year old girl asked, "Why do you wear pants and have short hair?" I answered, "I always cut my hair for heath reasons and because I like feeling free and fresh. I wear pants because there are mountains here. In the mountains some may be watching when I am bending or climbing, so I feel better and freer with trousers." Then she asked, "Why don't you have a husband?" I said, "My husband died, and I do not want another one because I chose for my children and me to be free, too."

All this has been a way of rejecting me, but I endured, thank God. I have endured by reading more books, especially about women pastors who are marginalized in different places, both in Latin America and elsewher.e I discovered the women pastors in the Bible, who walked with men, like it says in the book of Luke. Well, I guess they were pastors, both for their family and the community where they lived. I read and reread the Letter to the Romans, and thought about the many women pastors Paul mentioned. All this gave me strength and helped me to resist.

Upon arriving here, I thought I was going to return to Peru and my family stayed there, waiting. But here I found safety, whereas in Peru the situation was extremely difficult with the political clashes, the Shining Path guerilla movement and all that. There were car bombs near my family's home. The military raids were constant because my neighborhood was a center of guerrilla concentration. In my daughter's school, in Puente Piedra, the guerrilla blew up a portion of the building. There were death threats against pastors. At night we were watched by the military because they banned meetings. And the others banned us from being near the military. So all this was terrifying for my family and me, and my mother was elderly. So, I decided me to go to the office of the United Nations High Commissioner for Refugees and talk with them about the situation. They asked me to bring the letter sent by my daughter, which I had in my purse. Then, I had the opportunity to be accepted as a refugee and bring my family here.

We didn't move to Los Guidos immediately; first we lived in Alajuelita. To survive, I began to work as a seamstress. Then, the church called me, through professor Alonso Ramirez. I responded to that calling, because the church was without a pastor.

Well, here there were also difficulties, like in Peru, for being a woman, for cutting my hair, for wearing trousers. But I have not gone away, because it's not much to say "go away". I have not heard it myself, but the attitudes of some people say, "get out of this community." I have been in the organization of pastors from the community for eight years now. In the beginning, the men never called on me to pray, or speak. I sat patiently. Only one pastor accepted me, but everyone else did not, because I would go, modestly, without fancy clothes, just plain clothes like ordinary people, and the men would wear suits and ties. Even being in a poor community, they showed off, but I sat there and it didn't take long for somebody to ask "What is this lady doing here?" Well, the pastor who had invited me said, "She is the pastor of the church of Guidos Five." It has been eight years and just recently they have asked me to preach. Now they say, "Pray, sister, lead us, tell us of this ministry, what are you doing?" It is recent, but it took many years to speak to me or even address me.

I have dreams. I dream of the transformation of this community where I work and serve. I dream of a world that is free from the sort of violence that I have experienced and that so many others suffer every day.

And, yes, I would encourage people to study theology, especially women. My generation has opened doors, we have worked hard to create spaces where people have learned to accept us in ministry. If Christ is calling someone to serve, either as a minister or a lay leader, I would encourage him or her to take advantage of every opportunity that presents itself to learn to do better whatever it is that he or she is called to do. Who knows where Christ will lead?

Janet W. May, Editor | **Portraits**

Julio Murray
Panama, Episcopal

My name is Julio Ernesto Murray. I am Panamanian. First of all, thank you for the opportunity that you give me for sharing a little of the many experiences that have led me to the ministry that I am doing. Right now, by God's grace, I am the bishop of the Episcopal Church in Panama. I also have the opportunity of serving my brother bishops in the Central American Episcopal reion as the vice president of the House of Bishops. Very recently I am learning to fulfill with dignity the presidency of the Latin American Council of Churches. I am married to a Costa Rican, Ana Lorena, y we have two children. We live in Panama City.

How did I come to study theology? I have to give you a little background. I am a graduate of the Panama National Institute, a high school with a revolutionary heritage and history of struggle in Panama. When I finished high school, in 1976, I entered the school of medicine of the University of Panama and studied in the program for two years. I realized that this wasn't what I was looking for. So, I tried out my second interest, a technology program. Thanks to God, I earned a diploma in computer systems analysis and this diploma and level of training made it possible for me to work for the Bank of Panama for five years. My job, as part of a team, was to assure the transition from manual to computerized systems. So, in terms of analysis and engeneering, we did that job.

I had the special opportunity to visit Chicago as a participant in an event for young Episcopalians. One night when I returned to the dormitory, it turned out to be a special night, one that transformed my life. I had an experience like Saint Paul. No I didn't fall off a horse, but yes, I clearly felt the presence of the Lord Jesus around me and showing me that this was the moment to follow him. I have been a member of the Episcopal Church since the cradle. My grandparent's were founders of what today is the parish of Saint Christopher in Lefebre Park, in Panama City. In their home there were always many activities for raising funds for buying supplies and reconditioning the church building. So the church practically began in my grandparent's home and I grew up with all that. I was the first youth to have the opportunity of serving on the board of the Saint Christopher church, as well as being in youth groups, serving as lay leader and youth leader, all while I was still working at the bank. I never stopped going to church, since this was the focal point for a great many activities of my life. But that night was super special; I felt that God gave me a vision and called me, and I knew it was time to say, "Here I am, send me".

Upon returning to Panama City, I talked with my priest who at that time was Bishop Clarence W. Hayes, now deceased. He began with me the process of vocational preparation. The most interesting part was when I arrived before the parish board. I had to appear before it. I was a member of the board, the youngest member. When I told them that I was preparing with the Bishop to begin theological studies, they all stood and sang the Doxology, giving thanks to God. I didn't understand why they did that. They prayed and then were seated. I asked why they did all that, and they all looked at me and said, "We've always seen you as a priest, it's good that you too finally have seen it and accepted!"

Another question is why did I study theology at the Latin American Biblical Seminary? This also is interesting because, coming from an Episcopal cradle, I had the opportunity to study in an international, interdenominational seminary. I believe that this is due to the foresight of Bishop Hayes. He had at that time a vision of autonomy for the Anglican Province of the Central American Region, but didn't have anyone prepared in Latin America to work in Latin America. All my predecessors and other persons came with experiences from other seminaries of the denomination that were in the United States. But having someone prepared in Latin America to work in Latin America was a first. In second place, it was the time that Latin American theology was at its high point, that is, of theological production. Conjunctural analysis and all biblical-theological aspects that were occurring at that time were really important to the church project the Episcopal Church was proposing. For this reason, the bishop thought it really important that I received the best theological formation that the region offered. I also had had the Latin American Biblical Seminary recommended to me by a former student, Rev. Carlos Enrique Fiesta, an Episcopalian from Guatemala.

He highly recommended the seminary and had no doubts that it was where I should study. In having the opportunity to study in the Latin American Biblical Seminary, some said I was an experiment by the Episcopal Church, and that later I should go to a denominational seminary.

After returning to Panama, things changed and there were other necessities. We worked with what the seminary gave us; it was always an interesting challenge. I feel that, as an Episcopalian, the Latin American Biblical Seminary made an immense contribution to my theological and pastoral formation. I feel that the seminary gave me the opportunity to accompany many friends at the seminary with the learning I was receiving. I didn't have to wait to return to Panama or return to the local church in order to be sensitive and capable of pastoral accompaniment. In San José I worked with Episcopal Churches and had the opportunity not only to put into practice what I was learning, but to live pastoral accompaniment. From the Good Shepherd Church in San José, and also the Saint Mark Church in Limón, the Holy Mary Church in Siquirres and the Saint Luke Church in Pocora, I had the opportunity to share with youth and adults. Later, thanks to God, upon returning to Panama I had the chance to serve in the Bocas de Toro region.

I feel that one of the things that most impacts my ministry and is a product of my work at the Latin American Biblical Seminary, is the model of priest that I could develop. The priestly model that I knew was that of an office, where rites were prepared, visitors received, and everything else was done. But my time, experience and formation in the seminary prepared me for something different than the traditional ecclesial profession. I profoundly felt that it gave me instruments and a capability to be a missionary priest. This for me was very important because I had the opportunity to carry out ministry in the streets, in homes, in the neighborhood, in women's groups, youth groups, and with men. The Biblical Seminary gave me tools so that I could analyze the historical conjuncture using biblical-theological and pastoral knowledge that was relevant, so that people could understand that life revolves around the fullness that Jesus offers and that meaning in life comes from participating in the Reign of God. Although the signs may be few, when we are able to relate to others, and to understand that Jesus died and arose for us and that his life project for us is for today, we receive the power to dream and to construct this new reality in the present. It is this reality of the Reign of God, in terms of justice, equality, inclusion, respect for human dignity, of knowing that all of us, although we are different, are in this same plan and package together, I believe I would not have been able to know and do if it were not for what the Latin Amnerican Biblical Seminary taught me.

Portraits! | Janet W. May, Editor

Julio Murray

I was able to learn to confront a number of disconcerting things that didn't support life; I was able to learn about the social dimension of the church. Thanks to my learning at the seminary, I am able to continue to research, as well as to combat racism and discrimination. I am an African-descendent. My grandparents came to build the railroad and to dig the canal. They dreamed of one day returning to Barbados or Jamaica. I do not know Barbados, I do know Jamaica, but I was born in Panama, in Central America, I am Latin American. I'm not going to betray the birthplace of my ancestors and what they taught me I will always preserve. I will pass it on to my children, but I was born in this place and nothing can separate me from this reality. The Latin American Biblical Seminary helped me cement this Latin American identity as an African-descendent because I came from a background that gave much importance to Antillian roots and traditions. But I am an African-descendent born and raised in Central America and that has other connotations, and so I am going to be involved in all aspects of Central and Latin America that are important for promoting life. Everything that goes against life, I will denounce and I will announce the truth. So this is the way I translate what I learned at the seminary. I am not only an office worker or an administrative priest. I am one that works in communities, with peasants, with women, black people, indigenous people, and I believe that with each of these we have been able and have had the good fortune, to help them be able to identify that each has made important contributions toward constructing a reality that promotes life and demands an end to death.

Among my dreams, I always have perceived that God would give me the opportunity to be the servant of thousands of people. I don't know when, but I feel that God is calling me to this.

I would like to offer some advice to the Biblical University. I believe that one of the areas where we must make a significant contribution is stewardship of creation. We are suffering from global warming and we haven't done much in the churches to raise awareness about the need to change the way we do things. I believe that this must be done through local churches, but we also have to be prophetic before the leaders of our governments.

I believe that another piece of advice that I can give is that just as there are opportunities for theological meetings, there should also be the same opportunities for pastoral meetings. Seminaries don't make pastors, but pastors need a place, a space where they can share experiences and help others who are beginning their ministries and now are walking with us. I believe that the work the Biblical University does regarding gender and inclusion is important; I believe that the preparation of the directors of the various study centers is vital. Increasingly the Biblical University will face the challenge of preparing an integral leadership for the church, be it lay or clergy, in Latin America and in many other places of the badly-named Third World.

I feel that increasingly the Biblical University will feel the challenge of not only teaching what Jesus taught but also making real the promises that are fulfilled by following and obeying Jesus as Lord and Savior. One doesn't know if one is good or not while studying, but when one has the chance to put into practice what one learned, that is the real test. I have no doubt that if what I do is seen in a good light, it is because I am responding and accompanying a felt reality, a reality that our people live. I expect to continue contributing a grain of sand through my work with indigenous people, Afrodescendents, and peasants, against discrimination and racism, but also through the opportunity of being a leader-servant that contributes toward building God's reign from this corner of the vineyard that God has given us.

Portraits! | Janet W. May, Editor

Élida Quevedo

Venezuela, Pentecostal

My name is Élida Quevedo. I am working in Venezuela. I come from a national Pentecostal church, the Pentecostal Evangelical Union of Venezuela, in which I have been working since I was fifteen years old; I also work in theological education at a campus that is in connection with the UBL, called Pacto. I work as a professor of theology and also in the area of academic administration.

My pastoral experience in the church has been very diverse. First, I worked a lot in the areas of liturgy, working on the formation and training of liturgical teams with churches, supporting our national church and the region. I have planned and led liturgies for many national and regional activities. For three years, I have officially been the pastor in a small community in Maracaibo. The interesting thing about this pastoral experience is that we have been forced by circumstances to work in pastoral teams. I am the official representative of the church, for matters that require it, but in reality, several pastors do the work. We divide the work by consensus, we plan as much as we can, and that allows us to be able to develop in other fields, meet other obligations, and carry out other activities without neglecting the church. Initially, it was difficult for the church to accept that kind of job sharing, but now they value it and feel very good about it.

The decision to study theology was circumstantial. I admit that at first it was not my choice. I began to connect with the church and with the leadership of

Portraits! | Janet W. May, Editor

Élida Quevedo

the church from a very early age and, when I married one of the church leaders, young at the time, but the son of the church's founders, I began to develop a vocation for community service. This opened the feeling of necessity for training and preparation in order to serve better, and that is when the possibility presented itself. We were offered the opportunity to come here to the seminary in San Jose for training, and to me it seemed like an excellent opportunity. I felt like it was God opening doors and giving me the opportunity I needed to be able to better serve my church.

The difference is tremendous, because an subjective, intuitive experience has become a reflexive experience, very important, that empowers the church itself. It is not the same to have an untrained leadership, whose ignorance is shared with their communities, than to have trained leadership whose contributions are solid. It helps the church to have leadership that is formed, and personally, the experience has been truly enriching. It helped me to grow personally. For me, the theological training I received has been very, very important.

As an example of the way in which I do ministry differently because of the opportunity I have had to study theology, I can tell you about an experience I had after the Integrated Seminar called, "The presence of God in the midst of suffering." The contributions of Pastoral Psychology as a science in recent years have been very, very important and I have applied them in more than one way working in pastoral care, above all with people that have been through situations of great loss, who do not deal with them as they should, whose lives are sometimes in a hole because of poorly treated situations of conflict. I have found that the lessons we have learned in many of the courses that we take here in our training process have been truly helpful to the people we serve and work with. I have many examples and every day I thank God for what I have learned and can do because I can help people with problems more effectively. We have been able to help break the journey from despair to hope, by applying what we learned in the classroom. We have learned that books do not say everything, but experience alone doesn't say it all either. We have to do a mix between what the books say and what the reality of experience says.

As a person, I have a dream of continuing my personal training process. I am currently working on a master's degree in social work, with the idea of linking all the teachings of theology, pastoral care, and the Bible to community work from a social intervention point of view, using qualitative research methods. I hope I can help and work in a comprehensive manner with the communities. My dream is to be able to move forward in my personal training process, and also be able to strengthen a Venezuelan educational project that is rooted in the process that is actually being lived here. At this moment we are working hard on that and building an educational proposal that is relevant to this reality we are living.

I would encourage people who feel called to study theology, in any form whatsoever. That is, there are many ways to train for the ministry or any kind of work within the church or in communities on behalf of faith. It is important to have the best possible training, because only then can we become truly relevant. With robust training, like what we have received here at the UBL, it is contextual, ecumenical, integral. I would encourage people not to study at a traditional school of traditional theology, but in a program that serves you, is stimulating and that is sound, like this one.

Portraits! | Janet W. May, Editor

Janet W. May, Editor | Portraits

Blanca Viracocha

Ecuador, Methodist

My name is Blanca Viracocha and I'm Ecuadorian, from the Methodist Church. I was in charge of a local congregation in Ecuador that has been a very nice experience. Twelve years ago I was handed this ministry and it has been a very nice experience to work with the community, seeing the need to live the Gospel everyday, not to separate everyday life from God. We opened the doors of the church to support the community in literacy campaigns, medical brigades, and in the processes of community meetings. Previously, it wasn't done, church doors remained closed and were only opened on Sundays. There have been many changes in the church.

I have always been in church. Since I was young, I supported work with boys and girls, or whatever I was asked to do. Then I saw the opportunity to study theology. Despite the many unknowns that I had in terms of biblical texts, I felt that the Bible didn't always say the same thing as the way it was commonly preached. Before, I could not challenge this because I was told that it was word of God. I wanted to study theology because of these unknowns, to see if it was true what they told us, and to understand how social ideology is based on theology and how those in power have used theology to dominate others. These things have drawn my attention, so I am studying to understand them.

I began to study theology because of the missionaries Eunice Arias and Luis Aramayo, who were in Ecuador. They made it possible for there to be a UBL extension in Quito. There was already the site of Riobamba in the indigenous community, but because it was so far from Quito, Eunice and Luis did the formalities to open a campus in Quito. There we began studies. Studying at the UBL has been a great blessing for me. I would not have been so happy to study in another seminary with another theological perspective. The UBL has opened many horizons for me because one of the things I like most about the UBL is that it helps us to understand God in everyday life, in reality and not stay there, and to question why God does not agree with injustices. That has helped me greatly in opening ministries in the community, not keeping the church locked up until Sunday for singing, but to live the gospel beyond the church, with our close friends, helping in the struggle for change in our community. That is what the UBL has taught me.

One specific impact of studying theology was to confirm that theology is lived in the ordinary and is in the earth, that we are responsible as sons and daughters of God to look after what we have, to live responsibly as human beings in society, and as part of God's creation. It also helped me in terms of gender, it has helped me a lot to improve the status of women in my community and that's why I fought for literacy in my community. I saw many results and I felt very satisfied.

My great ambition is to complete my bachelor's degree in theological studies. Then, I would consider another specialty, to serve the community in the best way possible. My greatest desire is to organize my community to create micro-enterprise projects for youth and women, and manage this so that the community will grow economically and in social health.

My advice to those who wish to study theology is that it is a good option. I highly recommend the theological perspective that the UBL offers, if you have such a vocation, then you going to feel very accomplished, as I have felt. In closing, I would like to thank God, the organizations and people who supported me, and the teachers who have shared their knowledge in these years of study.

Janet W. May, Editor | Portraits

César Llanco

Peru, Methodist

I am Cesar Llanco Zavaleta, Peruvian and Methodist. Currently I am working in the Methodist Church of Peru. I have the appointment of chaplain to a Methodist school of about 1,000 students in Huancayo and I am also a pastor at a local Methodist Church, in an area called El Tambo. It is a church of about 50 members, more or less, and I also have the responsibility of the San Pablo Seminary, an ecumenical seminary in Huancayo.

My ordination was in February, but since 1992, I have already been working in the church. My first appointment was as a substitute minister, as a call before being ordained in the area of the mountain forest. I was in a rural church, San Gerónimo, for two years. Then I left to study in 1994. In 1995 I returned again to another rural church, called Concepción. So I've been doing pastoral work for a number of years.

My decision to study theology came to me when I was fourteen years old. My father is a Methodist pastor and since I was ten I identified with his work. I was always involved because the church had assigned a car to him and I always went along. My dad's work was in the south, for seven years in Chincha, Ica and in that area. These were areas of great needs. The church was always in marginal neighborhoods. Then, I saw that my dad served four or five groups apart from a main church. He told me that there weren't enough pastors to do the work. It was then, at fourteen, in a marginal neighborhood, I said, "I'm going to study theology." I was in my third or fourth year of secondary school and already knew very clearly that as soon as I finished secondary school I had to go to the seminary of the Methodist Church to become a pastor, to be just like my dad. That's what I remember; I saw great need and a pastor who served four or five groups, and of course it was clear to me that more pastors were needed.

In 1988 I began to study at the seminary in Lima. This gave me a better understanding of what it meant to prepare for ministerial work. On the way, I became involved in educational work, first at the Methodist School, teaching classes in religion and then in theology. There were others who encouraged me to continue studies beyond the seminary in Lima. I was already beginning to work in what was San Pablo, in Huancayo. My view was broadened to see that there are other areas where the theology is exercised beyond the local church. It was about 1997 when I began to make efforts to come to Costa Rica, and in 2000 I arrived at the UBL. From there, my understanding has not changed regarding the ministerial work that I have been called to do. I still feel called to serve the local church and also contribute to academic training.

Studying theology has helped me better understand what God wants for human life. It has helped me to understand the meaning of the calling to serve the Reign of God. Many churches are very conservative and their understanding of the Reign of God is very abstract, very distant from reality. But studying at the Seminary in Lima and even more in the UBL, helped me find this broader dimension of what it really means to be called to the Reign of God. It has already transcended the boundaries of the church, because it is the whole community and can encompass different tasks in different places. Also, studying theology has helped me understand the importance of tolerance and respect, because sometimes we in the church have the legacy of a selective or sectarian thinking within the evangelical atmosphere. In this regard, the UBL provides an important ecumenical experience. Even though the Methodist Church in Peru is ecumenical, often it is only in theory. It is in those spaces that the theological training has made this contribution.

The UBL has helped me develop another concept of the pastoral and ministerial work. Many times, the church pastor is perceived as a docile person who does their job quietly, depending on what the institution wants. In our studies in the UBL, we have discovered that ministerial work has a prophetic role and there are many things in the church that have to be said out loud, that have to be denounced. So, I am not alone, but already some who have left the UBL have voiced concern within the church, have said some things that that the institution does not like. For example, in 1998, a bishop took me out of the assembly for voicing a concern. He said I was not the pastor that the church needed because I asked questions in the assembly that he and the superintendent didn't like. So, I feel that this has been a marked influence among many other experiences in this training with a different understanding. Pastors also have to ask questions in the church, and not just accept what the institution says. I think that is where there is a significant contribution.

My wife Karina and I now have two areas of ministry. One is the local church as a community and institution and the other is the environment of academic training. At that level, we dream that what we have received can be shared with other colleagues in the communities of the central zone. There isn't an ecumenical space in the central region except for the San Pablo Seminary. So, we want the seminary to grow and for the brothers and sisters to rethink their understanding about the dimensions of the Reign of God, what the announcement of the Reign of God means. We also want this seminary to be firmly established. That is our dream, to consolidate this project. With regard to the church, we dream of a different church, maybe not the entire institution, but at least the communities that we can work with and help them become more involved in the daily reality that surrounds them. That is the level of our dreams.

There are several young people who have talked to me about the possibility of studying theology. One of the things that I said is that they think about it, because while today's theology may have a more academic training as a profession, there is a difference. It is a career or a profession, if they want to call it that, but of vocation and commitment. That is something that I always say to them, think about it well before entering seminary, because when you leave you will have different areas to work in, not just the church. There may be other places in the community. But beyond thinking about the resources that they can get, they should think about what they can give, because faith calls us to serve the community, to accompany it. We want to broaden the understanding they have. So vocation and commitment is something that we always explore when addressing this question.

Portraits! | Janet W. May, Editor

Luzmila Quezada
Peru, Wesleyan

I am Luzmila Quesada Barreto. I am Peruvian. At this time I am studying in the doctoral program at the Institute of Higher Education in Theology in Sao Leopoldo, Brazil.

I began to do volunteer work in ministry at thirteen years old. I was the leader of the adolescent youth group. When I was in high school, I participated in a high-school level student movement. As time went by, I found myself leading youth in the whole region of my church in Peru, the Pilgrim Wesleyan Church. I finished all that when I graduated from high school.

My father was a pastor and I didn't want to be a pastor for anything in the world. I said that living on faith didn't sit well with me. Nevertheless, the next year I was studying in a seminary. I said that I was going to learn more about teaching young people, but I'm not going to be a pastor. That was my idea. The third year, the leaders of my church said, "Sister, you have to go support a local church with your skills." This congregation had recently undergone a split. Since I had experience in youth ministry and the majority of the membership was young, they thought I was the ideal person to go there. I worked very hard in that church for a year, brought the congregation back together, and then when the church was back on its feet, filled with couples and families, plus the youth, the church leaders sent a pastoral couple. They said that a young person on her own couldn't handle that church, that I would need help, that now this was a family church.

So, I finished the two years of theology studies that I had left pending, then finished my bachelor's degree and went out and started a new congregation with a style of its own, a democratically led church. I put together a pastoral team and trained young people to work together. All of my pastoral work was with young people. I trained them in administration, music, Christian education and such. Along with this, I had a paying job because the church was not able to pay me anything nor did it fill my need to be in service. I felt the need to work in social movements. My pastoral work was "for faith" and I didn't receive any salary. So I worked half time in an ecumenical institution, where I participated in social movements. The first year, I was a secretary and the institution was called the Christian Center for Development and Service (CCDS). But another institution had recently begun. So, the CCDS and the Training Center joined together. We worked in movements of women, with the "glass of milk" program, with community soup kitchens. My work was half time with the church and half time with social organizations. I stayed with this for about nine years. Even while I was doing all this, I felt a need to take time and sort out all that I was doing. I was very active and never took time to sit down daily and think, because there was so much to do.

At the same time, I was saying to the church that it needed to work more with the social movements, but I encountered much resistance from the church leaders. However, they kept inviting me for further conversation. They said, "Sister, you are the one who does all this because you are the best trained among us. You have more experience." So, I think I stayed in my denomination because they respected me and my experience and wanted to stay in dialogue. I have tried to stay within the church, but to keep my eyes open to what is happening beyond the church. I have tried to share my ideas and not let myself get pushed aside. I have sought to maintain my freedom to ask questions. I think this has been one of the ways I manage my relationship to my church as an institution.

However, while I was working with the social movements, there were many difficulties because of the violence. I was an advisor to the coordinators of the "glass of milk" program and there were problems because many of the workers had received death threats. When they were threatened, some of them withdrew. I remember that when we visited the workplaces, we went at night. Sometimes we couldn't go to these places in daylight because we were being watched. We had to take precautions, many of us. One time I was photographed while I was in a meeting. The institution I worked for found out about these photos and was very worried. There was a lot of persecution going on against advisors of non-government organizations that worked in favor of human rights and that opposed political violence. So the institution told us to always go out in pairs, to take care of ourselves, to sleep every night in a different place. It was hard, but we had to keep going on. We always carried our identity documents with us, so that if anything happened, our bodies would be identified. This was back in 1991, when there was a lot of repression going on.

That was the same year as the Cholera pandemia. I was the health coordinator, coordinating between the "glass of milk" program and the religious and educational centers. I was also the coordinator of non-governmental institutions that worked at the local and district level. There came a time when we ran out of money and had to stop. I had reached a point where I wanted to continue my theological education; I wanted to study in the UBL. I said to myself that this was a good moment for me to do that. So I made plans, and then the office called and told me that they had found money to reopen the programs. But I said, "No, this is my opportunity to study, this is a time to work, but from the perspective of pastoral theology."

I came here and what a first month I had! I was always having health problems, because working with the church and with the social movements left me very little time to eat and to sleep. Logically, my health had suffered. During the first month, I said to myself, "My God, how can they be having all these discussions when people are dying?" But Mireya Baltodano* was really supportive of me and she helped me to stop and think about all the political violence that was going on in my home country. But we didn't just talk about the political violence, but also a series of violent things that had happened to me as a child. I wanted to escape, but I knew that that was what I would be doing, to avoid the pain. You have no idea how therapeutic those two years were that I spent at the UBL. It gave me a real opportunity to work things out. I did my thesis with Elsa, on "Popular theology with Peruvian women". It was a way of drawing together all I had learned and experienced in my years of ministry in Peru, and to identify the pain and suffering. For me, this thesis was the culmination of a period of confrontation, sistematization and renewal. For me, this is the point of a theology of daily living in the midst of violence, that even destroys our bodies.

When I returned to Peru, I decided to create a pastoral training center that dealt with aspects of corporality, gender, violence, these things that we don't like to talk about. That's why I formed the Kairós center, as a space to reflect on gender relationships. The first month that I was back, I held meetings with other

Mireya Baltodano is a professor at the UBL. She is currently serving as Dean.

Portraits! | Janet W. May, Editor
Luzmila Quezada

women theologians and proposed that we form a women's ecumenical roundtable for reflecting on gender, theology and pastoral ministry. They asked, "But how are we going to do this if we're not theologians?" I said, that we are theologians of daily living. So we opened up this program in Kairós and later we opened up a school of Gender and Biblical studies, as a diploma program. Until then, there had not been any opportunities for formation in Bible and Gender or in feminist theory. We opened a space for women pastors. Then we opened a program on women and citizen's rights, to struggle against violence against women. This was all followed up with Indigenous theology and a program on the pedagogy of caring, taking into account the writings of the Colombian author Luis Restrepo. Then I decided to do a master's degree and I told them that I was going to study issues related to body theology. Now I am continuing those studies at the doctoral level, incorporating themes of empowerment, creating spaces to develop our strengths, redefining power as something that we build together. I think there is a lot to be done.

My dream now is to finish my doctorate and have a space where I can do research. Many of our institutions offer little time and a thousand things to do, not leaving much opportunity for interdisciplinary dialogue and thinking about what where we need to be going. My dream is to open a center for research in an academic setting.

As a word to people thinking about studying theology, I would say, "Walker, there is no trail. You create the trail by walking." One of the things that we have to think do is think big and for that we need to train ourselves. We have to use our intelligence, our imagination, our strengths, to work to make those dreams become real. Now there are many ways to acquire training: virtual classrooms, extension programs, residency studies. Now we can no longer say that educational opportunities aren't available. We have to take advantage of these opportunities because through them we can grow and support each other.

Janet W. May, Editor | Portraits

Germán Alanoca

Bolivia, Methodist

My name is Germán Alanoca Mamani. I'm a Methodist from Bolivia. The Methodist Church is present in fourteen districts. I've worked in nine of them. When I assumed pastoral work in the provinces, I really had the opportunity to share my experiences and studies. There I had to put my studies into practice, because the church, in some districts, also has educational programs, such as the high school in the Yungas Disrtict. I have served as a church authority as district coordinator and I also have pastoral experience in rural, urban and suburban areas.

In my urban pastorate, the elderly people liked me. There I had 80 old people in need of accompaniment. It was really an experience, and I learned a lot. I believe that being a pastor is very beautiful work, a commitment not only to God, but to the people with whom you are working. This has strengthened me a lot. This year, I am president of the National Conference of Pastors, so I'm in charge of 45 pastors, and so in this way we continue to carry on this ministry.

I decided to study theology following a family experience. I converted to the church when I was twelve years old. At that time my sister was sick. I had learned some biblical texts. I took my sister to the doctor who said there was no cure, but I trusted in God, I placed total confidence in God. My sister was ill, almost paralyzed, for eight months. One morning the pastors visited my sister, laying hands upon her, and then we went to the market. When we returned, my sister was not in the house. We looked out toward the church and saw her walking toward us. We were greatly surprised and then we broke down. This is the testimony that really took over my life and I realized that I had to talk about it. It was then that I decided to become a pastor. When I began my pastoral work, it wasn't easy. I remember that we began studies in the hospitality center, when Rolando Villena was bishop. I had studied for three months when the bishop said, "Please, go back to your churches. We have to suspend everything here." Well, after that, the program was reorganized and I finished the bachelor's degree. Now I'm in the licenciature program and I'm still working with the church.

Since there was no university-level theological program in La Paz, the Methodist Church, the Aymara-speaking Lutheran Church and others worked together to organize study groups. The missionaries Janet and Roy May brought from Costa Rica, in 1982, the list of students that were in the distance program (PRODIADIS) of the Latin American Biblical Seminary. They had the idea that all those students should join and study together. Teacher Janet took theology courses when she and Roy were in Costa Rica, following the military coup by Garcia Meza and that's where they learned about PRODIADIS. Pastor Roy contacted others who had similar interests, among Methodists as well as other denominations. A team of teachers was organized. It included pastor Roy, Dr. Jorge Pantelís, Fanny Geymonant de Pantelís and pastor Matías Preiswerk in La Paz, and Mario Rivas in Cochabamba. Teacher Janet taught classes in Research Methodology, but also served as the Academic Registrar, in order to be sure that our documents were organized properly for the Biblical Seminary. This was the beginning of what we called the Center for Theological Studies (CET), and the La Reforma Methodist Church let us use the lower floor for classes and an office. Later, CET was reorganized as FAET (Theological Education Faculty) and then ISEAT (Andean Ecumenical Higher Institute of Theology) which is the actual institution. I've been a part of all of these stages.

Studying theology helped me in various areas. One thing is that it helped me to do theology from the grassroots, doing theology in different areas, such as the struggle for land, or the march for dignity and territory. Also we have accompanied communities as they have thought about their religious convictions from the perspective of Andean theology. As a pastor who works in these communities, I have had to do theology from these real situations and my studies are resources that serve as tools for exploring them. I am grateful to the Latin American Biblical University because it has helped us move into these new areas of academic theological formation.

Now, the Methodist Church in Bolivia is in a process of transition and I expect that the theological studies so many of us have done in ISEAT and the

UBL will serve us well. One of the things that Roy taught really impacted me, and that was about bioethics and God's creation that we are not caring for. We talk about water, deforestation, and erosion that are all happening. Study materials about this for use in the communities are urgently needed. This is a pastoral challenge and I'm going to talk about this in our church meetings. Also, we are a diverse church. In Bolivia there are 36 different cultures. Perhaps not all are part of the Methodist Church, but we are trying to widen the vision of the church and its mission in order to share these urgent concerns in relation to health and the care of life.

Regarding youth who wish to study theology, I believe that as a pastor I should accompany them, to know what their purpose and commitment really are. We have a study center that is very appreciated in Bolivia: ISEAT. Students even come from other countries to study with us because they want to know how to do theology from the grassroots. We share with them and they really are able to see our alternative theological vision. In relation to our brother and sister youths, the church is supporting them. The church has many possibilities for promoting the preparation of others, not just youth but also to be concerned about questions such as gender, because the sisters also need to be prepared. ISEAT is open to all, not just the evangelical churches, but also catholics. In this way it reaches out to all who are interested.

Portraits! | Janet W. May, Editor

Germán Alanoca

Yolanda Rosas

El Salvador, Guatemala and Bolivia, Mennonite and Pentecostal

I am Yolanda Rosas. I am Salvadoran by birth and also Bolivan by marriage and in my heart. My husband and I work with ISEAT, the Andean institute of theology that cooperates with the UBL. My work focuses on Pastoral theology. When I graduated from the university, I began working in pastoral theology and just one month ago I assumed responsibility as the academic director of ISEAT and the university-level program. I also work in the Pentecostal church and what is called the Latin American International Council. This is the denomination into which I was born, so I have returned to my roots and I am very content with that. We work in a zone where there is much poverty. We hope to construct a building that will serve for worship, but also for community service, especially with children and health programs.

Before coming to Bolivia I already had a lot of experience elsewhere. I am Salvadoran, but when I was 14 we left El Salvador and went to live in Guatemala. My parents are missionaries. There was a wartime situation in our country and we stayed ten years in Guatemala. I think that it was there that I began to have my first ecumenical contacts through an insitution that was called the Conference of Evangelical Churches of Guatemala. There, we worked with different churches in theological education. I coordinated the extension program and worked with a lot of churches. It was in Guatemala where I met my husband who was there doing a period of supervised ministry as a UBL student. Later, my husband and

Portraits! | Janet W. May, Editor

Yolanda Rosas

I came to study in San Jose and then we went to Bolivia with the Mennonite Church, worked some with the Baptists and now we're with the Pentecostals – a little bit of everything!

I think I had an interest in studying theology from the time I was ten. I began to take correspondence courses that some evangelization program offered on the radio. So, at twelve I already had various diplomas but I had a desire to learn more and when I was 16, I entered the Mennonite Biblical Institute. The minimum age is 18, but they accepted me. I was the only female student in the whole three years I spent there. At nineteen, I was already assigned a pastoral ministry. I finished my basic theology degree and the Mennonite church in Guatemala needed pastors. Then I enrolled in the school of theology at the Mariano Galvez University and focused on Christian Education, and I enjoyed that a lot. When I married, I decided that it would be good to gather all of those studies up together and transfer credits to the SBL, which is now the Latin American Biblical University.

I come from a denomination that has not given priority or importance to theological education. I thought it wasn't necessary. But now, at least some Pentecostal churches are realizing that their pastors need preparation. Because of these beliefs, my family didn't support my desire to study theology, but I observed problems in some preaching and pastoral accompaniment that I knew could be overcome with opportunities to study, especially in situations of counseling. I watched my parents in ministry and I am proud of them, but I also felt that they, too, could have benefitted from opportunities to learn new things, new tools that they could acquire through study. I think that study is a good thing because it enables people to make even better contributions than just learning from experience. It teaches them to reflect on these experiences, to draw upon the wisdom of others, and to use new approaches.

One example of this can be seen in preaching, and there's a lot of that going on in churches. We are constantly asked to prepare Bible studies and theological education has helped me to gather my ideas together, to consult dictionaries and concordances, to research the origins of words, to understand the cultural contexts that biblical passages developed in, and to try to find meaning for today. So preaching is not just telling simplified Bible stories to people and coming up with the same old platitudes, it's about passing on important knowledge, making things meaningful for people. Studying preaching has helped me to do this, and I have had similar experiences with pastoral care and counseling moments. We need to remember that people are not just in need, but that they don't need words of advice repeated from easy phrases taken out of the Bible. This doesn't respond to what they're going through. I enjoyed the pastoral care and counseling courses a lot. The practical experience provided a supervised opportunity to apply tools, to connect to people, listen to them and also to accompany them for lengthy periods. We give time for people to find their way through pastoral accompaniment, and they discover what they can do to confront their problems. All of this is through the pastoral interview, listening and moving step by step with them. I enjoyed learning this.

As for dreams, what I would like to be able to do is write. I don't have time for thinking about writing with all I am doing with a family, two jobs and many responsibilities in the church. I don't have the time to sit down, reflect and write what I know about Christian education or about gender. And I know that we need teaching materials in these areas!

I would like to encourage people to study theology, especially women. I would like to tell them some of my story, tell them what it has meant to me, to my family and the changes we have undergone, thanks to theological education. I would like to share with people from other places and traditions and encourage them. I would encourage them to enroll in a seminary program and to question themselves, because not everything they learn in seminary is easy to assimilate. The opportunity to study makes us question ourselves and what we do, it challenges our beliefs and our faith. A person who wants to study theology should know that their foundations will be shaken. I would like to think that these people will find much to do in their churches and beyond their churches, because often when people talk about ministry they say things like, "I don't want to be ordained, I don't want to be a pastor, I don't want to put up with this struggle to be ordained, like you and many others, particularly women, have done." Well, that was my calling, my vocation and I had to struggle, but here I am. There are many ministries in the churches and there are also many other spaces where we can put into practice what we learn in theological education.

Portraits! | Janet W. May, Editor

María do Carmo Moreira Silva
Brazil, Methodist

I am Reverend María do Carmo Moreira Lima, a Brazilian of African descent, and an ordained pastor of the Methodist Church. I am better known as Pastora Kaká.

Without a doubt, my pastoral ministry has been different and this has brought me difficulties with the church as an institution, but it has also opened doors to building more ample relationships. Since the beginning of the 1990's, as a seminary student, I have spent time on the streets of Rio de Janeiro, acompanying boys and girls, adolescents and women who live on the streets.

In 1993, I had some difficulties with the local police. I was with a group and, in the process, I assumed responsibility for a young person who had no family. I was arrested and I got acquainted with the reality of the spaces dedicated to detaining young people who were accused of criminal activity. Since then, I have been able to work freely on the streets of Rio with the support of the police authorities. We have made great progress in the work with this social sector.

In 1995, with five other women, we began a group called AGAR-the Black women's theological society. We have organized reflection groups, encounters and other activities to work on issues of gender, racial-ethnic discrimination and theology.

I began my theological studies in Brazil, motivated by a friend who is a pastor and also a theology professor. As I advanced in my studies, I went to Costa

Rica in order to participate in a program called the Sister Network, sponsored by the World Council of Churches. That is how I found out about the Latin American Biblical Seminary and I realized how important it was to reevaluate my own studies in relationship with my experience in community work. I decided to drop out of the program in Brazil and travel to Costa Rica. Our Father-Mother God knows our deepest desires! I managed to get my life organized, find money for a scholarship, and, with the help of some miracles I even got a plane ticket. So, I began my studies at the Latin American Biblical University.

Of course, not all of this has been easy! It was an enormous change in my life and in my pastoral commitment. It was important to be able to study full time, enjoying the opportunities I had to share what I was learning with professors and other students. It was important to live in a student residence hall with others from all over Latin America and from all different churches.

I learned a lot in every activity that the UBL organized. We enjoyed visits from famous theologians; we had many a "salad luncheon" in which we all ate together as a community. We had lunches and dinners in faculty homes, shared triumphs and pain, and many other things. All of these things helped me see how important it is that theology gets mixed up into real life. Or, better said, life is a theological reading, because our God is a companion who reveals himself in daily events and we discover him present in our midst, very simply and directly.

Returning to my home country, I was challenged to be coherent with what I had learned in the classroom and university life. For me transforming and expressing that learning concretely was a challenge. I felt that my ministerial work was more consistent and mature. But it wasn't easy! Little by little, new opportunities opened up and new experiences affirmed that I was learning to put my faith in action. I returned with the certaintly that youth and working women had to be empowered, to recognize themselves as active participants in their reality and with their own struggles for liberation.

My commitment to the good news of God's reign has also found expression. In 2003, while Benedita da Silva was the Governor of the state of Rio de Janeiro, I was invited to work as a special advisor to the Secretariat for Human Rights. On this occasion I received the honorary title of Citizen of Rio. Actually, I was born in Minas Gerais. This was an affirmation of my work with marginated populations. On this occasion, being the only woman honored, I was also invited to give the main speech for the event.

At this time, I am confronting a very delicate brain surgery. I am pushing my limits, but I keep working. I live being a woman and being black to the fullest, developing my alternative pastoral ministry. Often it is hard! But I continue.

I have a dream of developing a pastoral ministry that is therapeutic and that incorporates liturgy as a therapeutic experience for women who have been victims of gender and domestic violence, especially for those who have suffered violence within the church. I know this won't be easy and I don't know how I will be able to fund this work or to confront the political reactions within the institution, but it is important to have these kinds of encounters. At the same time, I would like to have some time to systematize in writing what I have learned from all of my pastoral experiences. I don't know how this will come about, but we'll see.

In my time as a student in different places and countries of Latin America, I have perceived that racial prejudices are the same regarding poor people of African ancestry, and especially regarding women who are African-Latin American. We carry burdens of many people's prejudices, many preconceptions that annul our affirmation of ourselves as protagonists. I have also seen that theology can also be a "little house" with very narrow walls. It isn't easy! It is a hard struggle, but Jesus affirmed that in the house of God there are many rooms! So, we must continue forward!

Portraits! | Janet W. May, Editor

Janet W. May, Editor | Portraits

Margarita Lais Tourn

Argentina, Waldensian

My name is Margarita. It is also the name of a very dear and quiet aunt who gave birth to twelve children and still is alive, taking care of her grumpy husband. It is the name of a great-aunt that, with her strong character and firm hand cared for the family farm. It is the name of saints and queens, of friends and of people I have never met. It is the name of the metal wheel (Daisy wheel) used in some electric typewriters. It is the name of a simple and rustic flower in my homeland in the south of Argentina that opens its blossoms on the same month as my birthday, revealing a golden button surrounded by white petals.

I have a name that was chosen for me. I know I am unique, but, sharing this name with so many others, seeing the infinite possibilities of my name, it is easy for me to realice that I am connected to other people and to all creation.

Years ago I left behind the local church ministry, the community responsibility as a full-time commitment, and periodical moves. I moved to the countryside. My new responsibilities are canning fruits and vegetables, supervising the farm, even giving classes to young people and preparing materials for discussion and reflection with different groups.

My father was a pastor and my mother was a teacher. I grew up in a family that lived simply, with an austere faith and the confidence in modernity that taught them to believe that the best inheritance one can give your children is a good education. Maybe that is why I always feel like my education is unfinished, that I need to read more, even though at times I become distracted and my feelings and activities also feed my thirst for knowledge.

As an adolescent, I had many interests. I was interested in art, communication, health … The country was emerging from years of chaos and a dictatorship. We were avid to participate, to create. I chose to become a pastor because it seemed to be the best way I could contribute. I still affirm that intuition.

I was very young when I began to study theology. It was a wonderful time of learning and discovery and it gave me knowledge and a road to follow as I grew into a young adult. My faith was consolidated and solidified, leaving behind childish acritical beliefs. My faith began to develop a sense of wisdom.

I married, had a daughter and a son, did my supervised ministry perid and was ordained as a pastor. Everything I had learned fed into what I did in ministry. But, I also confronted challenges that told me that I needed to continue learning and that my pastoral experience alone would not teach me everything I needed to know in order to grow in ministry.

When I was doing my supervised ministry, I went with three companions to visit in the homes of people who lived in poverty. It shattered my very protected view of reality. The visit with a young woman of my age, loaded down with children and suffering from a facial paralysis as a result of domestic violence, along with other pastoral visits, challenged me to want to share a sustaining faith that would be received like fresh water.

It was after several years in ministry that I found at the SBL the resources I needed to reflect upon gender issues in ministry. My faith was strongly tied to a sense of justice and concrete liberation.

I continued in pastoral ministry and this complemented my classroom learning because it brought me face to face with death and failure. I knew how to fullfil the requirements to pass a course in a classroom or through distance learning, but I had no idea of what to do in certain concrete situations that escaped from my hands, leaving me with a feeling of helplessness and indecision. How could I appear to be effective when I wasn't, or didn't feel like I was? My faith, like the salty water of the nearby ocean, kept me afloat even though I didn't make any effort to swim until I could see the coast and find redirection. Mine was an inexplicable faith of one who experiences the maternal caring of the Holy One.

Various years went by and I built a space for myself along with recognition for my work that, taking into account my location, brought me to an ecumenical world filled with challenges and further learning. I was the pastor in traditional communities and I worked with the organization of youth ministries for my denomination. I had to learn to move around in a world of popes and politicians. And, I spent many evenings sitting by a campfire and accompanying others in their faith.

Always, the tenderness, critical thinking, hunches and surprises accompanied me. Life continues to reveal that when we are ready for something, reality shifts, and we need to be both firm and flexible to encounter whatever comes next. When we know the answers, the questions change.

Like many others who dedicate themselves to the experience of learning, reflecting and pastoral ministry, I have acquired baggage that shapes my life, that distinguishes me from others who share my name and brings me into encounter with other realities.

My dream is that we might look out over the balcony towards the future, rooted in the mystery of divine love, seeking wisdom, justice and liberation, as we are embraced by Tenderness humming us a lullaby.

Other publications of the Latin American Biblical University

ECCE MULIER
HOMENAJE A IRENE FOULKES
Escuela de Ciencias Bíblicas, UBL
UBL (2005), Price: US$11.00, plus shipping

This work is a tribute to the teaching ministry of Dr. Irene Foulkes, who, for five decades has combined academic rigor with spiritual sensibility. One outstanding aspect of her ministry was her incalculable effort to promote the role of women in the continent. Irene has been a teacher, a pastor and a friend of generations of women theologians, biblicists and pastors from many different countries, extending beyond the Americas and the Caribbean. This anthology is a collective way of expressing our gratitude to a teacher and a friend.

EL LIBRO DE RUTH
José Enrique Ramírez-Kidd
UBL (2004), Price: US$20.00, plus shipping

The book of Ruth makes a valuable contribution to biblical thinking. It gives theological status to daily reality, to little things. We discover a different face of God in the Old Testament: a God who is near, filled with intimacy and tenderness. The God of Israel becomes present in the decisive action and words of two women, one is the companion and the shadow at the right hand of the other. This study of the book of Ruth focuses on three moments: the exegetical process (analyisis of the text and study of sociological themes); pastoral (reflection on different aspects of the reality of everday experience and faith); and liturgy (the silent appropriation of the text, drawing upon liturgical symbols).

EN LA DISPERSIÓN EL TEXTO ES PATRIA INTRODUCCIÓN A LA HERMENÉUTICA CLÁSICA, MODERNA Y POSMODERNA

Hans de Wit
UBL (2002), Price: US$16.00, plus shipping

This first volume of work by Dr. Hans de Wit extends over 500 pages of the history of biblical interpretation, beginning with the rereadings of the texts that are found in the Old Testament, moving through the interpretations of the rabbinic and patristic periods, the period of development of historical methods, and postmodern biblical interpretation. The study and critical analysis of biblical interpretation prepares the way for the second volume, pending publication, in which different methods will be applied to the study of Judges 4, according to Dr. de Wit's proposals of complementary exegetical methods and hermeneutics.

VIDA Y PENSAMIENTO

Vida y Pensamiento is a semestral publication of the Universidad Bíblica Latinoamericana. It presents articles in the areas of biblical studies, theology, pastoral theology and related disciplines, in dialogue with contemporary Latin American reality. Each issue focuses on a specific theme from diverse perspectives.

América Latina:
1 año: US$16
2 años: US$28
3 años: US$40

Other countries:
1 year: US$20
2 years: US$36
3 years: US$52

For more information:

Librería
Universidad Bíblica Latinoamericana
Apartado 901-1000
San José, Costa Rica

www.ubila.net

Portraits! | Janet W. May, Editor

¿Would you like to know more about the UBL's non-degree study program?

You can find information at www.ubila.net. If you have questions, contact the university vice rector (nidia@ubila.net) or contact a center in your country.

Janet W. May, Editor | Portraits

¿Would you like to know more about the UBL's degree-level study programs?

You can find more information at www.ubila.net, send a messaage to the Academic Registrar's office (Registro@ubila.net) or contact a center in your country.

Portraits! | Janet W. May, Editor

Would you like to support the UBL and its work?

Online donations can be made at the following two websites:

The Advance
Advancing hope in Christ's name

Advancinghope.org
Project numbers: 09139A and 10247B

PCUSA.org
Project numbers: 865533 and 344202

Made in the USA